The New

CEO

TY WIGGINS, Ph.D.

Russell Reynolds Associates

The New
CEO

Lessons from CEOs on How to
Start Well and **Perform Quickly**
(Minus the Common Mistakes)

with Justus O'Brien, Laura Sanderson, Margot McShane, Rusty O'Kelley and Stephen Langton

WILEY

Published by John Wiley & Sons, Inc., Hoboken, New Jersey.
Published simultaneously in Canada.

For general information on our other products and services or for technical support, please contact our Customer Care Department within the United States at (800) 762-2974, outside the United States at (317) 572-3993 or fax (317) 572-4002.

Wiley also publishes its books in a variety of electronic formats. Some content that appears in print may not be available in electronic formats. For more information about Wiley products, visit our web site at www.wiley.com.

Library of Congress Cataloging-in-Publication Data:

Names: Wiggins, Ty, author.
Title: The new CEO: lessons from CEOs on how to start well and perform
    quickly (minus the common mistakes) / Ty Wiggins.
Description: Hoboken, New Jersey: Wiley, [2024] | Includes index.
Identifiers: LCCN 2023058448 (print) | LCCN 2023058449 (ebook) |
    ISBN 9781394244348 (hardback) | ISBN 9781394244362 (adobe pdf) |
    ISBN 9781394244355 (epub)
Subjects: LCSH: Chief executive officers.
Classification: LCC HD38.2 .W54 2024 (print) | LCC HD38.2 (ebook) | DDC
    658.409–dc23/eng/20240123
LC record available at https://lccn.loc.gov/2023058448
LC ebook record available at https://lccn.loc.gov/2023058449

Cover Design: © Russell Reynolds Associates
Author Photo: © Georgie Clarke

For my children Taj, Ash, Aja, and Mataya.

I love you more than can be expressed by all the words, in all the books, in all the world.

Contents

Foreword

Your first year as CEO is arguably the most decisive period in your entire CEO journey. It is when you make your mark as a leader—signaling to your organization and the market that you were not only the right choice, but that you have what it takes to lead the business to even greater heights.

It is a time when you showcase your intentions as CEO and set the stage for the bold moves that you will ultimately be remembered for—and will shape your legacy for years to come. A fast and impactful start is critical.

Yet, as I know from my own experience becoming CEO of Wolters Kluwer 21 years ago and as a board member witnessing other CEOs in transition, your first year is also a time when your resilience and adaptability is truly put to the test.

If you can quickly get to a point of strength, navigating your organization's complex dynamics and earning the trust of your many stakeholders, you will prove your mettle and rise above. If you can't, you may find that you spend the rest of your tenure trying to recover.

When I became CEO, my burning platform was clear: to reverse Wolter Kluwer's poor performance and lead the company forward in the digital age. I was excited by the challenge ahead. And having already run Wolter Kluwer's American division for a few years, I was clear on where we needed to go. I knew, however, that rallying the organization would not be so straightforward.

There were, of course, skeptics who didn't believe in my vision and doubted that Wolters Kluwer could be transformed But I knew two things to be true: First, I had been given a chance. And second, I didn't have long to prove I could do it.

One of my biggest pieces of advice is to surround yourself with the right people. Know your strengths and the strengths of those around you. Find people who have skills that you don't. And bring people together to make sure they function as a team. Communicate clearly—and often. The mantra of *"Say it and say it again"* is mission-critical for every CEO in transition.

And always remember that no matter what you think before becoming CEO, you'll never be 100% ready. Be humble enough to acknowledge that and commit to becoming a life-long learner. However successful you are, there will always be something new to discover.

Since I began as CEO, the world has changed significantly. Navigating this complex moment in history will require transformational CEOs who have the vision and passion to make an immediate impact. I cannot think of a better moment for Russell Reynolds Associates (RRA) to share the inside track on how to get off to a strong start as a new CEO and set up yourself for long-term success.

Ty Wiggins has made it his career to help new CEOs deliver a strong start. He distills his rich experience in this trusted step-by-step guide that will help you tackle the issues you face during your transition. Whatever your situation, his advice works. This is a critical book for all new CEOs—and those who work with them—and it could not have come at a more important time.

A CEO transition is not for the faint of heart. But those who are willing, and able, to embrace both the opportunities and challenges that lay before them will leave an indelible mark on their organizations. So, step boldly into this transformative journey. Although it will be demanding, the rewards will be immeasurable—for you, your team, and your business.

Nancy McKinstry, CEO and Chairman of the
Executive Board, Wolters Kluwer

Introduction

If you are reading this book as a newly announced or appointed CEO, congratulations!

You are about to embark on something that only a very small percentage of the population ever gets to experience—to lead an organization and all of the people who call it theirs.

Perhaps you're already in the role. Perhaps you're getting ready to start. It may be your first time being a CEO. It may be your third. But whatever your circumstances, this is a time of great celebration.

This moment is about recognizing years of hard work and ambition (and, I'm sure, a fair bit of sacrifice along the way). It's a time when you are at your most energized to execute your vision of a brighter future for your organization. And, of course, for you and your family, too.

Enjoy this feeling. You've earned it. And the reality is that you'll need to keep returning to this place when times get tough. Commonly, that is a *when*, not an *if*.

Much of what they say about the CEO role is true: it's complex, confusing, and often exhausting. This is the most challenging and loneliest role in business (just how lonely is often what takes CEOs by surprise). The scope, gravity, responsibility, accountability, and exposure of the CEO role are unparalleled.

I probably don't need to remind you that, as CEO, you're not only responsible for your organization's strategy, but also for its financial viability, and long-term sustainability. You're also responsible for the livelihood of its employees (and their families), and in many cases, your suppliers and partners (and their families, too).

You have no doubt read that CEO turnover is at an all-time high. Our research shows CEOs across the S&P 500 and FTSE 350 lasted an average of 7.6 years in their role in 2022, compared to 9.2 years in 2018.[1] And you're no doubt familiar with the numerous stories of CEOs who didn't make it past the two-year mark at organizations like HSBC, Procter & Gamble, Apple, Boeing, and Hewlett-Packard.

If CEOs fail, especially early in their tenure, the consequences can be vast. When Fiona Hick, the CEO of Fortescue Metals, one of Australia's largest companies, stepped down after six months in the role, it immediately wiped off 4% of the share price (approximately $1.5 billion at the time).[2]

The tremendous amount of pressure and enormous responsibility is why so many people don't seek the role, and are happy to stay as a key contributor to someone else's strategic vision—and that's fine. We can't all be in charge.

If the responsibility of the role scares you, that's normal. If it didn't, I would be concerned.

The trick is to now walk the tightrope over the complex web of feelings and experiences you'll inevitably face as a new CEO, nimbly stepping between decisiveness, confidence, self-awareness, and empathy to execute your vision and unlock the most life-affirming move of your career.

Why I Wrote This Book

As cliché as it will sound . . . because people told me I should.

I have one of the best jobs. As a leadership advisor and global lead for the CEO & Executive Transition practice at Russell Reynolds Associates (RRA), my job is to guide

CEOs the world over through their first 12–18 months in their new role. Sometimes I'm their coach; sometimes, their cheerleader. Often, I'm their venting partner. More often, I am their challenger and sounding board. I am always their trusted advisor.

The work I do—and the stories I'm privy to—is a true privilege. Having the opportunity to gain a backstage pass to so many CEO transitions, talking with leaders who are at the top of their game at a time when they're at their most vulnerable, has given me a unique vantage point into the good, bad, and ugly of CEO transitions. That's what I aim to share in this book.

Why? Because for all the attention given to CEOs, there is very little advice on how to actually land well in the early days and set yourself up for success. Walk past any airport bookstore and you'll find countless books about what it means to be a leader or a CEO, or how to nail your first 90 days as a general executive. What you won't find is a book that specifically covers the challenge you face now: the CEO transition (a period that, for the purpose of the book, covers your first 12–18 months in the role).

Successfully navigating your first weeks and months as CEO sets the tone for how you'll be perceived for years to come. Yet, until now, few CEOs have shared their stories on what worked, what didn't, and what they wish they'd done differently.

For years, I'd entertained the idea of writing a book to compile the rich experiences I'd gleaned advising CEOs in transition. It wasn't until one of my CEO clients stressed the point so emphatically that I was kick-started into action.

We'd been working together for a little over 14 months, navigating everything from an organizational restructure to a significant business sale. It had turned out to be a very challenging first year as CEO, and through the process, we'd developed a relationship that was honest, trusting, and at times, frank.

As we finished up our last session together, he said, "The way you have supported and challenged my thinking, added insights and examples at just the right time, and on more than a couple of occasions, told me I was flat out wrong has been invaluable. You should share all of this in a book."

I'd heard this a few times already over the years and told him so.

He waited all of 0.05 seconds and said in slightly richer language: "So, get off your backside and do it."

So, I did.

What You'll Find in This Book

This book is a combination of CEO experiences, observations, and research. It is written to give you a wide and disparate view of the transition from the perspectives of the CEOs who have done it before you *and* from my perspective as an advisor, having worked intimately with 50-plus CEOs across the world to ensure their success in real time.

Over the following pages, you will find the rich stories— warts and all—of global CEOs who have successfully managed their transitions—and who have graciously agreed to be featured in this book. CEOs like Whirlpool's Marc Bitzer, who shared the memorable piece of advice he'd received early on that "you'll have 10 really bad days as CEO—you just don't know when they happen." Or Carol Tomé, the CEO of UPS, who said as CEO you stand at the crossroads of multiple contradictions. "You rarely get a clean shot at things. More often, you face a paradox, or a series of decisions and judgment calls where you are picking the 'least worst option.'" Or André Lacroix, CEO of Intertek, who told me that "there are very few leaders who can really improvise on the spot effectively, so the rest of us have to be very well prepared."

To supplement this experience, and solve for any confirmation bias I may have, I also completed detailed interviews with 35 CEOs across public, private, and private equity (PE) organizations in 2023. A concerted effort was made to ensure these interviews were a mix of internal and external appointments, from a range of industry sectors (13), and with backgrounds across seven functional disciplines. A third of the CEOs I spoke with were women. All CEOs were interviewed between 12 and 18 months in the role, so they had both the benefit of currency and hindsight. Interviewing them at such a critical juncture in their respective CEO journeys forced them to truly reflect on their approach, actions, and decisions during their transitions, and most importantly, answer off the cuff. These are some of the unnamed stories you will read in the book. We also surveyed almost 200 CEOs globally about their experiences transitioning into the role.

When I think about how to summarize a CEO transition, the mental picture that often comes to mind is a parachutist flying through a tight canyon. Parachuting is not like driving a car. When you toggle left and right in a parachute, it doesn't create an instant or neat reaction. It creates a pendulum effect—and you need to work hard to keep adjusting to find the right momentum. This, to me, feels like the most apt description of what it means to be a CEO in transition.

A constant process of fine-tuning to avoid hitting the walls, until you finally emerge in open skies, where you can really perform and deliver.

The nature of CEO transitions makes it hard to have a one-size-fits-all, clear, repeatable roadmap for success. Instead, what I do with clients (and what I aim to replicate in this book) is work through the key expectations, decisions, challenges, risks, and opportunities that commonly arise.

I have distilled this into 10 components that, in my experience, make for a successful CEO transition (see Figure I.1).

FIGURE I.1 CEO transition success, Russell Reynolds Associates, 2024.

These 10 components inform the chapters that follow. While the ideas are presented linearly, the reality is that some clearly overlap, and others may resolve only to return again. My recommendation is to read the book from start to finish to get a feel for the learnings in their entirety, and then dip in and out to refresh on certain sections as challenges arise during your transition. The book has been structured to allow for this to happen.

Chapter 1 looks at why the complexity and scope of the CEO role can make your transition feel like an Everest-scale challenge. In that chapter, you learn how you will feel out of your comfort zone at the exact moment you need to be performing at your best and why, regardless of what you believe going in, you will feel lonelier than you've ever been. You'll also read stories that speak to the weight of the responsibility you now face as CEO and how the demands of the role are always more than you expect. As PepsiCo's CEO Ramon Laguarta told me, "When you're running a business unit or region, you can always ask your boss to carry the ball the last mile. But now *you* are the one who has to make the final call."

Engaging in robust transition planning will set you up for success, but no two transitions are exactly the same. So, what should your plan cover? In Chapter 2, you'll find how different factors can influence your early approach and success, including the influence of your predecessor (or ghost), the pros and cons of being an internal successor versus an external hire, and the state the business is in when you arrive. You also hear from Sanjiv Lamba, CEO of Linde plc, who had to throw away his meticulously crafted 100-day plan just days into the role, on why flexibility and agility is critical.

As a new CEO, you will never have complete visibility over what's happening—nor will everyone always tell you the truth. You'll need to work quickly to plug the gaps you have in context and detail. Chapter 3 looks at how to burst the CEO Bubble that you will find yourself in, including the benefit of being curious over being right, watching out for your biases, and some more obvious but overlooked aspects of your ability and willingness to really listen.

Next, the book takes a look at how to strike the right balance between patience and action. This is something that many new CEOs struggle with. You will face considerable pressure to move fast. While there is no formulaic answer to how quickly you should move, there are some aspects to strongly consider. I raise these in Chapter 4, which looks at why it can help to find early wins or common pain points to address (or as Stephanie Tully at Jetstar Airways called them, the symbolic acts). And why you need to be deliberate about your bigger moves.

What you say and how you say it sets the tone for much of your transition. Take time to get your messaging right. As Doug Mack, former CEO of Fanatics, said: "The CEO title has an unbelievable ability to move teams and organizations— it has to be taken with great humility and care." Many have referred to CEOs as being, among so many other things, the Chief Communications Officer. This is true in part. What you say during your transition and how you say it will either be an accelerator of your success or the complete opposite— as discussed in Chapter 5.

Such is the pressure of the role and the challenge of the transition that it is common for new CEOs to experience a crash during their first 12 months. They face a knock in confidence or a series of challenges that make them think hard about what they have gotten into. In Chapter 6, Alan Beacham, CEO of Toll Group, shares ways you can reach out for support to find your way to the other side. As the new CEO for your organization, the sheer number of tasks can be daunting. Your to-do list likely includes hundreds of items. So, here I also help you work out what to do first, second, third, tenth, and eighty-third.

The top regret I hear from new CEOs is that they wish they had moved faster on their teams. Chapters 7 and 8 explore how to do this as quickly (and safely) as possible. In these chapters, you discover how you can get a good read on your Senior Leadership Team (SLT)—or executive committee—through both gut instinct, as well as assessment data; why you will need "wide T-shaped leaders"; and why establishing a "first-team" mentality is so important. I also discuss the potential challenges in managing people with different thinking styles and the implications of consensus leadership.

Chapter 9 covers how to engage the board and investors in detail. The headline message is that you'll need to engage both the board and your investors early and often in your transition. A key learning is that this will take up much more time than you probably expect. In fact, the second-most common regret from CEOs, behind wishing they had moved faster on their teams, was wishing they had better engaged their board earlier. How you approach and work with the board is one of the markers of your success in transition and in the longer term. I discuss ways to do this, the common pitfalls to watch out for, and the areas where boards worry about you—their new CEO.

Cultural change is hard and takes a long time. Every culture has a positive side and a dark side. In your transition, you need to take the time to really understand whether the organizational culture will help you achieve your vision or work against it. In Chapter 10, Mark Clouse, Campbell's President and CEO, and others share how to come to grips with your culture—how you should assess it, work to shift it, and ensure it does not derail your transition.

Finally, Chapter 11 includes answers from the named CEOs featured in the book to the questions: "What do you wish you had done differently?" and "What advice would you give someone about to go through a CEO transition?"

Over the coming pages, you gain rare insight into the experience and voices of your peers (named and unnamed) and the benefit of (almost) everything I have found to be highly relevant to CEOs in this most challenging time.

What you *won't* find is a chapter titled "Strategy" or "Vision." While these are high (and critical) priorities for new CEOs, the intent of this book is not to be a guide on what you should do strategically (there are, fortunately, more than an ample supply of books on that topic). Where I can add the most value to you is to share the experiences of CEOs on *when* and *how* they approached this crucial topic during their transition, rather than *what* they did.

* * *

I realize that I am writing to an exclusive club that many never get the membership card to. Yet, it's a group that has a disproportionate influence on so many lives. The reality is that while the CEO role is unique, many of the transition and leadership lessons enclosed are also applicable to other senior executives, who sit one or two levels below the CEO, including first-time and returning C-suite executives and/or those who one day aspire to take the top job. The lessons and advice will also be helpful to founders and entrepreneurs and family-owned businesses, as well as those who work regularly with CEOs during their transition, including board chairs, directors, Chief Human Resources Officers, in-house counsel, and private equity teams.

My hope is that every new CEO, their board, and the team around them, will learn from this book—whether it's their first, second, third, or fourth time in the role. But more than that, I hope that every new CEO will be generous in sharing its lessons and their experiences to leave open the door for the next generation of CEOs behind them.

From the work I do every day, I know that the role of CEO is so demanding that you cannot do it on your own. You need help and you need support. Make sure that you have plenty of both.

It's an experience that I am lucky enough to guide others through—and now I aim to provide some of the same help to you. I hope to improve your success, and as a direct result, the positive influence that you will have on the lives of the people in your care, and the rest of us who need you to be successful.

And we all want you to succeed. We certainly don't want you to fail before you get that chance. My hope is that this book helps you in some small way with your success.

What It Means to Be a CEO   By Constantine G. Alexandrakis, CEO at RRA

It's never easy being a CEO. But those at the helm of organizations today have it tougher than most. This is something I had seen time and again when advising CEOs the world over during the past two decades with RRA. I knew how important transitions were and the challenges that many faced. Now, I've experienced this firsthand.

(continued)

I have been CEO of RRA for two years—an experience that has been rewarding and challenging, particularly as the world spins faster than ever before.

The reality is that the to-do list for any CEO is now much larger than it was before. On top of the perennial tasks of leading an organization—to set the vision, coalesce the organization around a new or refreshed strategy, and manage the financials—you must contend with a growing list of external risks, from economic jitters to geopolitical flare ups, and racial and social injustices.

Managing these immediate priorities comes at a time when you must also deliver on growing expectations to position your organization for long-term growth. Every CEO today knows *why* they need to embrace tech transformation and sustainability. What is less clear is *how* to do it. These are complex issues, for which there is no playbook and for which everyone is looking to you for answers.

At the same time, in a world of multiple stakeholders, media, and social media scrutiny, CEOs can no longer only focus on what they do; they also need to focus on how it will be perceived. This can create a considerable tax on time, constraining your ability to properly solve issues and drawing away much-needed mental capacity for long-term decision-making.

Yet, despite all the challenges, there is a dearth of information on how to get it right. From our vantage point as a world-leading leadership advisory firm, we know that these issues *can* be overcome as well as *how* to overcome them. Within the following pages, you will find exactly how to land well as a new CEO so you can build the strongest platform possible to deliver on the ever-growing expectations of the people you now serve. If you are a new CEO, or about to be, I highly recommend that you add this book to your reading list.

PART I

So, You're a CEO

CHAPTER 1

Why CEO Transitions Are So Hard

"Uneasy lies the head that wears a crown."
—Shakespeare, *Henry IV*

How can a role that is so visible, so carefully watched, studied, and written about, be one that is so hard to prepare for and get right?

Nobody goes into the CEO role with their eyes closed. You have likely been preparing for weeks, months, and possibly years. You talk to other CEOs, you read everything you can, you might find a mentor or coach. And when you head into the role, you're confident that you couldn't have done any more. Yet just a few hours or days later, you find out that nothing can actually quite prepare you for becoming a CEO.

The truth is that no CEO transition is without challenges. There's no singular reason for this. Typically, it boils down to a combination of the following factors.

Out of Your Comfort Zone

Ascending to the top job is a monumental transition. As Ramon Laguarta, CEO of PepsiCo, told me. "You think you know what it will be like, but you don't. It's a massive shift."

The Spanish native has served as CEO of the soft-drinks giant since 2018, after more than 25 years working across the company's European and North American divisions. He'd seen every corner of PepsiCo, working through periods of stability as well as turnarounds and acquisitions, yet becoming CEO still presented new unknowns. "The experiences I had from growing up in PepsiCo were very helpful," he reflected. "But when you become CEO, you find certain things are totally different to what you know."

One of these is the realization that you are the ultimate decision-maker. "When you're running a business unit or region, you can always ask your boss to carry the ball the last mile," he said. "But now *you* are the one who has to make the final call."

Ramon added, "Managing the board, the media, and investors—that's also new. Even if you have been exposed to them, you are not exposed the way you are when you are the CEO."

There's also the challenge of being the ultimate driver of a new strategic vision. For Ramon, this means pivoting PepsiCo toward accelerated growth, embracing a new corporate mission and vision, and positioning the company to become *Faster, Stronger, Better*.

"Even on the things that you think you know operationally, there's a step up in complexity," he said. "You're dealing with the globe versus a particular region, function, or category. Then there's the time horizon. When you're running a business unit or region, you're rarely thinking five years out, you're thinking one to two years maximum and you're much more focused on delivering now. As CEO, it's five years plus."

Throughout your CEO transition, you may find yourself feeling exposed and vulnerable, even weak as a leader. The state of change is so radical that many of your information networks and skills are temporarily blunted. It's a bit like driving a new car in a new country—yes, you are an experienced driver, but everything feels different.

It's also a time when you have an intense amount of attention and focus on your actions, your performance, and even how fast or slow you walk. So now, you're not only driving the new car in a new country, with different rules and conditions, but you also have people in there with you, scrutinizing your every move, and quietly thinking they could do a better job.

The result is that when you begin as CEO, you can quickly move from a position of strength, one where you have been performing at your best, to a position where you can feel out of your depth. This loss of "capability" can rock your confidence and self-esteem. It can be hard to find ways to steady yourself.

Alone in a Crowd

There are many misconceptions about being CEO. Unfortunately, the one about it being extremely lonely is not one of them. This is what CEOs most frequently tell me when I ask them what the hardest adjustment is about the role.

Carol Tomé was warned before taking the helm of global shipping company UPS that she would feel lonely. She wasn't fazed. "I would say, 'How lonely can it really be?

It can't be *that* lonely?' What I've since learned is that it is *extraordinarily* lonely," she laughed.

"When you are a member of an executive team, you hang together," she told me when we met. "Now, my executive team will wait for me to leave a meeting so that they can debrief together. It's the reality and you have to get used to it. But it is super lonely."

Being CEO is like being alone in a crowd: you are rarely physically alone and yet at times you can feel like the only person on the planet. An often-cited study from 2012 found 50% of CEOs reported feelings of loneliness, with 61% believing it hindered their performance.[1]

Loneliness can manifest in different ways. It's lonely intellectually as you no longer have any peers to spar with. Hopefully, you have a good relationship with your leadership team and the chair of the board, but it will not be the same. It's lonely in that there will inevitably be things that you know that you cannot share. It's lonely in candor as you can't just say whatever you're thinking anymore. And it's lonely emotionally—there are very few people with whom you can really share how you're feeling.

Sanjiv Lamba, CEO of Linde plc, is another CEO who found the role lonelier than he had expected. "I am the internal candidate, so I should have read the tea leaves," he told me, with a smile. "But you can't see it until you are there. It is just the reality of the role."

Sanjiv described how, at any given time, he can't talk to his leadership team about many of the things he's thinking about, even though he has complete trust in them. As he said, "It's just the nature of the things that you do as CEO and the decisions you are making."

One response is for CEOs to fight to feel part of a team, for camaraderie, and even a wish to be liked. But this causes knock-on issues as they struggle to separate themselves from their team. As CEO, you are surrounded by your senior leadership team, but you are not really part of it. You will need to regularly disassociate from the team in order to make the tough decisions that are necessary for your organization to succeed, short and long term.

The other coping mechanism is to further isolate yourself and become an island, which only blunts your decision-making, as well as your confidence in your decisions. Isolated CEOs can also start to doubt the level of trust and support from those around them. Unfortunately, it can be a downward spiral that makes a tough role even harder.

The Imperfect CEO   By Justus O'Brien, Managing Director at RRA

> When it comes to CEOs, organizations often expect candidates to be the full embodiment of excellence and success—to be perfect.
>
> They expect CEOs to avoid any missteps as they set the direction and strategy of the company, lead and develop the executive team, build and maintain relationships, make decisions, communicate effectively, manage financial performance, and demonstrate integrity and ethical leadership.
>
> High expectations of CEOs are nothing new—and historically, weren't a problem. But two trends over the last 30 years have moved the bar from "great" to "perfect."

(continued)

First, the rise of CEOs as public figures. Since the 1990s, the role of the CEO has become more public facing. Many of the most successful businesses of the last 30 years depend on bosses with big personalities and big visions, such as Bill Gates, Jeff Bezos, and Elon Musk. These celebrity CEOs create a public image of success that permeates other organizations. Second, the role of corporations in society has changed, *putting new demands on CEOs.* New demands keep emerging, like sustainability, Gen-AI, geopolitical uncertainty, and new approaches to data security. Yet old demands never drop off.

Striving to meet this level of perfection is not only unattainable, but it will also stand in your way of true success.

There is often a benefit to recognizing that you're only human.

When CEOs can admit their flaws and mistakes, they create a sense of trust and authenticity with employees, investors, and other stakeholders.

Imperfect CEOs can also be more innovative than leaders who focus on maintaining a perfect image. When CEOs are comfortable acknowledging their imperfections, they're more open to new ideas and ways of thinking.

And imperfect CEOs are more resilient and better equipped to handle challenges. By confronting their mistakes and learning from them, setbacks are less likely to derail them and they're more likely to bounce back from adversity.

So, rather than striving for perfection, aim to embrace your flaws and use them as an opportunity for growth and development. By doing so, the organization will be more authentic, innovative, and able to manage challenges—all essential elements of long-term success.

A Heavy Crown

When I ask CEOs about the best and worst parts of being CEO, they often give the same answer to both parts of the question: the responsibility.

"You realize there is no one else," Marc Bitzer, CEO of Whirlpool, the American manufacturer of home appliances, told me. "I'm responsible not just for financials, but for 60,000 people and their families. The buck stops here. If you think too much about it, it can paralyze you."

For many CEOs, the sense of responsibility extends in a meaningful way to their customers. I am yet to meet a CEO who doesn't care deeply about their customers. But, for some, the industry they work in makes the weight of that responsibility much more visceral.

Stephanie Tully, whom we meet again in Chapter 10, is the CEO of one of Asia Pacific's largest low cost carriers, which provides low fares services to approximately 20 million passengers each year.[2] "You're flying people every day, and you do everything you can, but you have to be ready for literally any situation," she told me. "I was warned at the beginning that you never sleep easily as the CEO of an airline."

When you are CEO, you are also in charge of making the decisions that no one else can make—decisions that often have significant ramifications for the future of your organization, its stakeholders, and many people's livelihoods. Yet, it is this total responsibility that most likely drew you to the role in the first place, the part that you accepted without hesitation.

Doug Mack, a three-time CEO, who has recently stepped down from the helm of Fanatics, which manufactures and retails merchandise for global sports fans, described the complexity of the job as sitting at the "pinch of the hour-glass," trying to manage the "insatiable expectations" coming above from investors and below from employees. Not to mention, "only the hard stuff ends up on your desk when you're CEO."

Doug added, "Anything straightforward, fun, or easy is solved by the incredibly talented people you have in your organization. All the stuff that comes to you as CEO are things that all those smart people already worked on, debated, tried to figure out, and they couldn't. When you're the CEO, you're signing up for that."

Of course, if you've previously held a C-suite or regional GM role, you'll have already experienced responsibility and accountability, especially around large decisions. You may have been asked to *sell-in* your point of view or been in the room when the decision was made. But the ultimate decision was made by someone else.

It's different when the proverbial buck stops with you: no one to defer to, no one to share the responsibility with, and no one to stand beside you shouldering any negative consequences. What makes this even harder is that many of the decisions you'll make as CEO don't have a definitive right or wrong answer. Some are judgment calls. Or, in other words, "Whatever you think, boss."

"There's lots of people to help and advise, but in the end, you have to make the decisions—it's a weight you can't put down," Lyssa McGowan told me after her first year as CEO of Pets at Home, the United Kingdom's leading pet care business. In her situation, the "weight" includes the jobs of 16,000 people and around £1.5 billion ($1.9 billion) of shareholders' money.

Before taking over at Pets at Home, Lyssa had spent years as a divisional leader at a major telco both as its Chief Commercial Officer and then its Chief Consumer Officer. It was some time before the lightbulb moment came that the CEO role wasn't just a larger mandate and that she couldn't just apply the lessons she'd already learned.

"I always thought that being a CEO would be, say, 30% harder than being a divisional leader, maybe 40%," she told me. "But it's not any percent harder. It has taken me a year to understand that being CEO isn't a *bigger* job, it is a *different* job." She continued:

> *Every week I'm making decisions where I've got three 'not great' scenarios and I have to pick the least bad one, or the one that I'm at least 50% sure is the least bad one. Then I need to perform alchemy and convince 16,000 people it's brilliant and amazing and we should all follow it. That's part of what it means to be a CEO—to create certainty and clarity where there is none.*
>
> *And when things go wrong now, I no longer have to convince my boss about the next steps, I have to convince myself. And it turns out I'm a lot harder to convince than any boss I ever had.*

To add insult to injury, the type of decisions that CEOs need to make often carry a time horizon that offers little opportunity for short-term feedback on whether you made the right call or not. You may not find out until months, years, or even decades later. It can weigh heavily on your shoulders.

As Ron Williams, former CEO of Aetna and current board director of Boeing, American Express, and Johnson & Johnson, told me, "It's important to recognize the multiple time horizons you operate across as CEO. You need to get today's work done today. You need to deliver for the quarter, and you need to deliver for the year. But most importantly, you have to build a sustainable institution for the next CEO to inherit."

What Honeymoon?

While you'll often feel the world is watching your every move as a new CEO, it is usually the case that you'll have a certain honeymoon period. If you're transitioning into a business that expects a turnaround, you may not feel this benefit. But for most other business situations, you'll have time to get up to speed.

Of course, you'll still be working through your honeymoon period. There will inevitably be things to do that can't wait—often many of these will have been parked waiting for you. But you will have the luxury of using this period to ask questions and really get to the bottom of what is going on (or has been going on).

It is also the period where the organization, board, and importantly, the market accepts that the problems in the business were not your creation. One day, they will be. Soon, you will cross a date where the attitude shifts and the sentiment is that you can no longer blame things on the "last administration." Knowing that this is coming means that you can take maximum benefit of it before it is gone.

Busier than You've Ever Been

A few years ago, I advised a CEO of a business in Europe, who had for years headed up the company's largest region, both in terms of workforce and revenue. He was highly regarded for his efficiency and his work-life balance and rarely worked weekends—something he had invested time in and was proud of achieving.

When he became group CEO, he was shocked at how much more there was for him to do. The increased demands were almost overwhelming. Having run such an efficient calendar as a regional CEO, when he managed 70% of the business, he was shocked to find that he couldn't stay on top of the requests for time, meetings, advice, and decisions.

For the first time in years, he was facing pressure from his family to manage expectations around workload. He had already found someone to take on his previous regional CEO role, had worked diligently in delegating, and saying "no," but it still proved to be a challenge that lasted for close to eight months.

The massive increase in demands on your time is often a significant shock for new CEOs, even those who have been extremely busy for much of their career. It is not only the complexity of the work and tasks, it is the number of people who want your attention. The board, which we will discuss later, can be a significant part of the increased demand on your time. This is one of the things you need to learn how to deal with quickly.

The reality is that you'll need to work hard to meet the demands of the role, and even with this Herculean effort, you still won't get it all done. The CEO role is one that you can't outwork. Getting more efficient, putting in more hours and weekends, just creates more work.

My intention is not to scare you with a portrayal of the challenges of being CEO. The truth is that there is no real sandbox for becoming a CEO, and as prepared as you are, there will likely still be areas or aspects that you do not expect.

Some of these things will be a pleasant surprise, others negative. But many will just be things that you need to deal with and make the necessary adjustments. The reality is while the previous factors outlined challenged nearly every new CEO I've worked with, every single one of them was able to overcome them, one way or another.

Common CEO Surprises

- **63% of new CEOs are surprised at the true state of the business.** Even with strong due diligence, it is often extremely hard to get a read on all the details of the business before you start, especially if the board's selection process leans on the optimistic side. Rarely do CEOs believe there was any intent to deceive. But it is common to hear the expression that things "aren't exactly as they were written on the can."
- **40% of externally hired CEOs are surprised about the reality of the culture.** They are disappointed, sometimes shocked, once they get into the business and can experience it firsthand. Often, it can be very different to how it was described.
- **36% of CEOs are surprised at the emotional weight of the role.** Most expect that they will be ultimately responsible for the organization and its people, the buck will stop with them, and they'll see the impact of their decisions and actions. But the magnitude of the role is still a surprise when it becomes a reality.
- **43% of new CEOs are surprised at the extent of required board interaction.** CEOs commented that

they were spending more time, attention and energy on the board than they had expected. For some, the time spent on board-related activities was so significant that it affected the CEO's plan of how they would allocate their time, resulting in stress as they struggled to execute early priorities.

Source: CEO Transitions: Defining Success in the First 12 Months. Russell Reynolds Associates, 2024.

One of biggest takeaways they all shared is: as CEO, your time is your most valuable resource. How you allocate your time is intrinsically linked to your success and impact as CEO. Early on this will be harder than when you are in the groove of the role. You need good support around your calendar—so you control it and not the other way around.

Some new CEOs are challenged by saying "no" to things. They are both trying to learn and wanting to impress. But with such a finite resource for such an influential position in the business—every minute must count.

Learning this lesson fast, Marc Bitzer, CEO of Whirlpool, found that he had to be firm with how his office handled requests for his time—telling them to watch out for, what he calls, "time cannibals."

"As CEO, everyone wants to meet with you, and you're trying to be nice, but my advice is to not accept. The moment you go for your first speaker conference, you'll get 100 other invites. So just don't."

"Be careful about how soon you want to join another board or a charity board because the time doesn't get taken from your work calendar, it gets taken from your family time or your personal time."

The reality is that there are so many opportunities to get distracted as a new CEO. And the dangerous thing is some of these distractions come in sheep's clothing.

"You know, they stroke your ego," Marc told me. "These time cannibals tell you, 'We need you, you're so important, you can add value to this meeting.' They don't come and say, 'Hey, we want to steal your time.' They package it nicely."

Seasoned CEOs

While there are obvious challenges the first time you do any-thing, the complexity and intensity of the CEO role means that even if you have done it before, and survived, it's still unlikely that the second time will be a walk in the park.

One second-time CEO explained it like this: "I played rugby when I was younger. Several years after my last game I was invited to play in a social match with work. I had for-gotten how much it hurt. It was the same with becoming CEO again."

If this is your second time as CEO, you have the benefit of all you have learned the first time around.

You have the gift of hindsight about what worked and what didn't. When you bring those lessons to your new role, you'll often work faster and with more confidence. But remember that your data set is limited. Don't let your previ-ous experience restrict your openness to new ways of doing things in your current role. Watch out for the "it worked the first time so it will work again here." Just because you turned left last time and it worked, doesn't mean you should turn left again.

When I work with seasoned CEOs, I often need to work hard to counter this self-confirming view as they look to find reasons why their current organization is similar enough to the last one for a particular thing to work. We are all desperate to be successful, and CEOs are no different. You will be enormously driven by the desire to succeed and working with something that has "served you" before will be very enticing.

In fact, there is an argument that the more experience an executive has, the more they are blinded by their previous successes and more inclined to decide an action based on past experience rather than the merits of the situation in front of them.

If it is your third or fourth time, you will be carrying even more "success baggage."

There is another nuance. In my research, seasoned CEOs were more likely to talk about the need to move faster on their team than first-time CEOs—something they said was a key learning from their previous CEO experience.

However, when we looked at how long CEOs took to make the first change to their SLT, first-time CEOs actually moved faster than seasoned CEOs.[3]

So, there's a difference between reflecting on doing something differently and actually doing something differently.

Just because you have been a CEO before, does not mean you will get it all right.

Source: CEO Transitions: Defining Success in the First 12 Months. Russell Reynolds Associates, 2024.

Never Too Soon for a Crisis

What can take a generally tough transition to CEO and make it much worse? A good old-fashioned crisis.

When you encounter a crisis in your transition, it not only challenges your organization, it can also derail your momentum as well as threaten your tenure. Different to a burning platform (which we discuss later), a crisis is exactly that: something that could severely damage if not destroy value to a level that is unsustainable or unrecoverable.

Covid-19 was a global crisis that affected not only the way CEOs transitioned, but also how they led their organizations and people through what was an enormous loss of life across the world. As tragic as it was, Covid-19 was a shared crisis—no organization was unaffected. While some prospered and others struggled, or even failed, the crisis landed on everyone. More often, you will experience a crisis that only impacts your region, industry, or organization.

Sanjiv Lamba, whom we met earlier on, was two days into his transition as the CEO of Linde plc, a leading industrial gasses and engineering company, when he had to deal with the full fallout of Vladimir Putin's invasion of Ukraine. This was not something Sanjiv had in his pre-planning. So, while you often can't predict what might happen, you need to be mentally prepared for the great unknowns.

Whirlpool's Marc Bitzer remembers only too well the advice he was given by a board director before he became CEO. "They told me, 'You will have 10 really bad days as CEO—you just don't know when they happen.' And it is true. You will have horrible days. The question is how to ensure you keep moving forward."

Marc added, "Now, seven years in, after Covid-19, a supply-chain crisis, and two wars, I'd be glad if it were only 10."

The New CEO Checklist

- **Accept your vulnerability.** Becoming a CEO is when you will be at your weakest as a leader. Recognize that you are not infallible and that you're out of your comfort zone. Harness your vulnerability; don't let it paralyze you.

- **Avoid becoming an island.** You *will* feel lonely as a new CEO. That doesn't mean you have to become isolated, too. Find support by growing your external networks—past colleagues, other CEOs as well as external mentors, coaches, and advisors.

- **Find trusted advisors.** Having people whom you can bounce ideas off, and who are comfortable challenging you, is essential. But due to your title and role, make sure you are turning to true confidants. They can be hard to find. Regardless, you need to find them.

- **Know that more is not always more.** The reality of being a CEO is that you can't outwork the responsibilities, tasks, and accountabilities. Protect your time—it's your most precious resource.

- **Get comfortable saying "no."** The demands on your time are extreme. How you allocate your time and priorities is critical. Saying "no" to requests and people will be essential—get comfortable with it.

- **Remember you can't know the unknowns.** But you can build your own resilience to dealing with crises by remaining adaptive and responsive to external events that have a material effect on your organization (and that will land squarely on your desk as CEO).

CHAPTER 2

Prepare to Win

"The will to win is not as important as the will to prepare to win."

—Vince Lombardi

In the 100 days before becoming CEO of Whirlpool, Marc Bitzer sat down and wrote his legacy—a 30-page document that set out exactly what he wanted to be remembered for at the end of his tenure.

The native German had been with Whirlpool for 18 years, starting in its European division as vice president, before climbing the ranks and moving across the Atlantic to head up Whirlpool North America, Europe, Middle East, and Africa—an experience that clearly helped him glow bright on the board's succession radar.

As he prepared to take on the CEO role in 2017, Marc took advantage of the countless long-haul flights he took with work to prepare his legacy document. He called it Agenda 8—a nod to the fact that he was the eighth CEO in Whirlpool's 120-year history.

The spark that lit the flame was a realization that becoming CEO meant he was now at the apex of his career—and there was no turning back.

"I realized that this is your last job. There is no promotion after this, so you might as well make it worth it and dream big."

Agenda 8 covered what he wanted to do from a company portfolio perspective, a strategic perspective, and a leadership perspective. As the document grew, and became more specific, he began to share it with both his predecessor and lead director in the interests of being "totally transparent" about what he had in mind.

Looking back seven years later, Marc is first to admit that he couldn't deliver on everything he had first imagined on those transatlantic flights. "With hindsight, it could be seen as a little bit like daydreaming," he smiled.

"It was not a strategic plan that would be created by a big consultancy. It was not a profit plan or an investor plan. It was what I wanted to leave behind. I wished that I would have approached every single job in my life with that mindset."

He continued, "Of course, you will never be 100% right. But even if I fall a little bit short, I will still have changed the company in some way."

The plan had another benefit: keeping Marc focused in times of uncertainty or difficulty. "You can call this document a vision, a legacy, or an aspiration in my mind. But it acts like a magnetic north. Even when it's dark, it keeps me going in a certain direction. And when I'm having bad days, it filters out the noise."

Plan

In my Ph.D. research, most CEOs told me that having a clear transition plan *before* beginning as CEO significantly impacted the success of their transition.[1]

A solid transition plan will give you structure, task direction, prioritization, and clear deliverables in your early days. This not only increases the level of confidence you have in yourself, but also the level of confidence the organization has in you, its new leader.

Your first couple of months will be a frenetic blur, and at times, you will want to reflect on what you have done, either for your benefit or in response to a question from the board or another stakeholder. Having a transition plan will make it much easier to answer questions around where you have spent your time and effort.

A transition plan is also a good way to flush out the real priorities of the chair and board. By presenting it early as the guide for how you will focus your attention, you create a situation where they can easily redirect you if needed. Remember that sometimes people find it easier to tell you what not to do than what to do. So, present definite ideas to generate a specific response, "yes" or "no."

André Lacroix, CEO of Intertek, a global company headquartered in London, England, that inspects, tests, and certifies organization's supply chains, is no stranger to transition planning. Recognizing that your odds of winning are often set before you start, he adopts a forensic approach to managing his early weeks and months in the role. "When you become CEO, preparation is the springboard for your longer-term success," the third-time CEO told me. "If you don't leverage the time before you start, it will be harder for you to perform as fast or as well as expected."

Every CEO will have their own approach to pre-planning, but for André, it starts when he first engages with the company, when he begins analyzing all the public information he can find. Once the offer is on the table, and André is in the twilight zone between accepting and starting, he begins meeting with leaders across the organization—something that only accelerates in his first three to six months. No stone is left unturned. "It starts with a 360-degree review of the opportunity, the size of the prize, as well as the organization's current performance, vision, purpose, and business model," he told me. "I also think about the value the organization places on delivering the customer promise, as well as its strategic priorities and enablers, and how I will work with the team."

This detailed investigation allows André to document his ideas for everything, from his strategic plan and onboarding plan to his "leadership script," which sets out exactly what he wants to achieve in his first 30, 60, and 90 days, as well as his communications plan for what he will say externally and internally at these key milestones. The final document is a day-by-day calendar of the first year. "I know exactly how I'm going to spend my time because time is perhaps my greatest resource," he told me.

Thorough testing of the ideas in your plans is critical—as André did. It can be helpful to stress test your plan with people inside and outside your organization so you can broaden your vantage point and ensure objectivity.

This was an approach that Hans Vestberg, CEO of Verizon, the largest telecommunications company globally, also adopted. His preparation for the role involved writing what he called Verizon 2.0, a detailed document that set out the changes he wanted to make to the business as it races to stay ahead of growing competition and build out its next-generation network, as well as how he planned to measure progress and spend his time.

Hans had a bird's eye view, having held the Chief Technology Officer role at Verizon for a year before becoming CEO. But getting the board aligned with his vision was critical—to not just ensure support, but to also avoid conflicts further down the line. "I wanted them to understand my thinking before they hired me," he told me. "I basically said, 'If you want to hire me, this is what I am going to do. I don't want you to tell me later on that I can't do something, or this was not how you understood that I was going to operate.'"

Once in the CEO seat, he was keen to test his transition plan. So, he created a think tank and tasked it with offering both objective and subjective viewpoints on his key projects, covering the organization's structure, its go-to-market strategy, and its culture.

The think tank was comprised of an external firm and an internal team that Hans deliberately asked to work on the projects concurrently, but separately, in an attempt to make sure his ideas were rigorously tested from all sides. "I didn't let the two teams talk to each other," he said. "I would bring them together every couple of weeks and they had the chance to listen to each other, and debate what they were thinking, but they ran with the challenges independently."

At the same time, he had one-on-one meetings with 256 of the organization's highest executives, in less than five weeks. "I knew what I wanted to do, but I wanted to understand how far away the organization was from what I wanted to do," he told me. "Plus, I wanted them to have face time with me, so they had the opportunity to tell me what they thought we should do as an organization. It helped them understand that the new guy has come in and he wants to listen."

This extended meet-and-greet included three questions: How should the company go to market? What was the organization really good at? And how should it measure success?

"Around 80% of what I wrote in Verizon 2.0 aligned with what people told me", he said. "Around 10% of the document covered things that were so far away that the executives weren't thinking about them yet. And the last 10% I had got wrong."

Effective Transition Planning By Rusty O'Kelley, Managing Director at RRA

Whether you are promoted from within or hired from outside, you will benefit tremendously from an orderly and thoughtful plan that the board encourages and reviews.

Unfortunately, too many CEO transition plans are an afterthought—something that's often only realized when things start to head south. At RRA, we typically advise new CEOs to adopt the following framework when documenting their plan. It covers six phases, which should be refined to fit the specific organizational context that you face.

Phase 1: Plan the Transition and Think about the Details

Working with the board, outgoing CEO, and hiring process owner (e.g., general counsel, CHRO, or trusted external advisor), develop a strawman transition plan that reflects your priority areas. The plan should include a clearly defined sequence of meetings, decisions, and communications to make the transition as smooth and transparent as reasonably possible.

Phase 2: Document and Communicate the Plan

Next, the transition process and decisions should be memorialized and communicated throughout the organization. During transitions, the leaders who sit one or two levels below you often feel the greatest anxiety. A clear communication of your process, and their roles and responsibilities, goes a long way to demonstrate stability and thoughtfulness to senior leaders and other stakeholders.

Phase 3: Build Relationships with the Board

To succeed, any new CEO needs to understand and engage with the board as a whole as well as with individual members. Meet with each of them one-to-one to develop solid relationships. Make the time to travel to them and share a meal. Get to know them as people and understand what shaped their views and how they think. This is wise even if you already know them—the dynamics of your relationship often shifts substantially now that you are CEO. You'll want to understand each member's expectations as well as the board's operating style.

(continued)

Phase 4: Share Knowledge and Cultural Norms

In the next phase of your transition, it's often wise to reach out to the outgoing CEO to learn about any important organizational relationships and the institution's culture. This is especially important if you've been selected from the outside, when a lack of cultural familiarity can lead to early missteps. Take time to understand "the way things are done around here." Internal hires should also prioritize this knowledge transfer as you're dealing with a greatly expanded network of constituencies now that you're CEO.

Your transition plan will need to be underpinned by a deep understanding of the company's goals and strategy, as well as the formal and informal elements of its culture. Focus discussions with your predecessor on the business and competitive environment, the strategy, the organization, its culture and its people—particularly the executive talent.

Phase 5: Learn Key Stakeholders' Objectives and Concerns

External stakeholders are more important than ever to all companies. Beyond just customers and regulators, today's world is more transparent, and stakeholders have the technology tools to focus on spotlight on your company. Get a handle around stakeholders and then engage the company's broader leadership group and key stakeholders to understand their perspectives about your vision—as well as the company's issues. This includes investment community, regulators, suppliers, key customers / distributors and relevant media.

Phase 6: Assess the Transition

The last element of a successful transition involves candidly assessing your progress against each aspect of your plan. Identify any problems and concerns that have arisen—and aim to resolve them quickly, if you can.

Adjust

While having a transition plan is proven to be an effective input in CEO transition success, it needs to be flexible, as Sanjiv Lamba found out the hard way.

After a lengthy and well-orchestrated succession process, Sanjiv had felt well prepared to take on the role as CEO of Linde plc, a global industrial gasses and engineering company that began life in the late 19th century as a pioneer in refrigeration. He'd been with the company 30 years, holding senior leadership positions across its various divisions and markets. In his own words, he'd written a "textbook 100-day plan." Sanjiv noted, "I'd read the books, and everyone said to me, 'You've got to have a great 100-day plan.' Then on day one I had to throw it in the bin, because I hadn't planned for Putin to invade Ukraine."

Six months before Sanjiv had become CEO, Linde plc had rung in a multi-billion dollar contract with Russia. It was a record-breaking win for the engineering division—the largest in the company's 140-year history. For Sanjiv, it was a positive signal of growth and a great indication of things to come. "I remember celebrating winning the business with my engineering team in Munich. They'd done a fantastic job, and we were all very excited. I had to meet with those same people after two difficult days of being CEO to tell them we were going to walk away from the contract."

To say Sanjiv felt blindsided by Russia's decision to invade Ukraine is an understatement. Not only was the entire organization looking to him for answers, but he also had "a thousand people telling me what I should be doing." Sanjiv said, "We were mindful of our teams in Ukraine. We were mindful of employees in Russia. But most importantly we call ourselves a company of values. I needed to be able to stand up and look at the mirror every day and say, 'Okay, I know we made the right call here.'"

This experience, early in his transition, when he thought he had a plan that would carry him, prompted Sanjiv to completely adjust his thought process about being a CEO. He began zeroing in on how to make sure that the company wasn't caught unaware by other developments around the corner. "It was tough. My 100-day plan would have worked well if the world had stood still. But the reality was our world had been turned upside down," he told me. "But even as I threw away the tactical 100-day plan, I doubled down on the communication ensuring every employee understood our priorities and why we made the decision we did. This is what aligned the organization and gave credibility to the messaging."

Before your start date, you exist in the unconscious incompetent stage (you don't know what you don't know). And as the military saying goes, "No plan survives the first contact with the enemy." Or as Mike Tyson, the heavyweight boxer, more elegantly articulated it, "Everyone has a plan until they get punched in the face."

The reality is that, in the world we live in today, the potential for leadership surprises is significant. From erupting geopolitical tensions to a global pandemic, we are facing situations that no one can predict. So, while you need a plan, you also need to be ready to revise it. At best, you'll need to adapt your plan during your first three to six months. At worst, you need to be ready to throw it in the bin and start again.

* * *

Another consideration when building your transition plan is to understand the specific state of play you'll soon find yourself in. It's one thing developing a plan in isolation, when you expect the path ahead to be bathed in sunshine; it's quite another trying to implement it if you've overlooked the risk of stakeholder resistance or cultural misalignment.

Ultimately, your transition to CEO is unique. Unique to you, your capabilities, your organizational context, and the wider business climate.

So, while your transition plan will need to pick up on CEO mainstays—your vision, your strategy, your immediate actions, and measures of success—it should also be mindful of several factors that will influence how you approach your transition *and* your early success.

Factors including the role your predecessor played (and may continue to play), whether you were an internal or external CEO hire, and the state of play at your organization when you take the helm.

Your Ghost

Your ghost is the former CEO who once sat at the same desk and in the same office you are now in. When the handover works perfectly, you'll have access to an outgoing CEO who is supportive, helpful, and happy to be moving on. They will work to ensure both you and the organization are set up for success. They will understand that you will see the world differently and that you will make changes. They will not only accept this but encourage it.

The good news is that this scenario does happen often. It's by no means an outlier. But *often* is not the same as *most of the time* and it's certainly not the same as *always*.

The unfortunate reality is that there can be situations when the outgoing CEO becomes a key issue to mitigate in your transition plan and consumes a considerable amount of your time, energy, and attention. Exactly how much time, energy, and attention depends on the reputation of the CEO you're following and how connected they stay to your organization.

Following a Hero

Death by comparison is the risk here: they were so great; you will never stack up; if only they were still here. While you are unlikely to hear these words yourself, it is almost certain that people will be saying it to each other.

When everyone in the organization thinks the former CEO was near perfect, it leaves very little room for you to make improvements. You may find you need to work harder "selling in" the changes you think will make a better organization, and you may find yourself fending off accusations— silent or otherwise—that "you're just doing that to make your mark."

The other challenge is that, over time, you may discover that all that glistened was not, in fact, gold, especially when it comes to the state of the business. This makes for a very awkward situation when you have to shine a light on the predecessor not being as perfect as everyone thought. If you find this to be the case, then tread carefully with how you disclose it. Use your newness to ask questions that point in the direction you need the board and organization to look.

Lyssa McGowan is one CEO who was able to come in with a change agenda despite following "a much-loved and very successful CEO." Key to this was avoiding any implication that what was done in the past wasn't working. "The previous three years had been unbelievably successful, and the business was rightly very proud," she told me. "So, I never talked about change—I talked about dialing up the things that were already there in order to deliver the new strategy. It wasn't that anything was broken, it was just that the world was changing, and we needed to change our strategy as a result." She added, "It was about communicating the vision for the future, while avoiding saying anything was broken or that we shouldn't be proud of who we are. It was an important balancing act."

Following a Villain

While this is often easier than following a hero CEO, it's not without its challenges. The trap here is that you get positioned as the incoming hero and it goes to your head. You find a willing audience to flog your predecessor, and you discover that you can buy extra time on their bad behavior and any resulting poor performance.

It is helpful when it is evident that the villain's decisions directly resulted in poor outcomes, making it abundantly clear that they "had to go." However, what if you find that the decisions and actions were the right ones or were necessary? What if you agree with them and would have made them yourself? Discovering the villain is not as bad as people made out is a tough spot to find yourself in.

Remember boards are groups of individuals who may make decisions based on bias, personal agenda, and personal preferences. It is not uncommon to realize that the board or executive team were, in fact, the problem and you're now at risk of becoming the next CEO scapegoat.

As with so many of the challenges you will face early, part of the solution is to be careful with your communication; be very deliberate with what you say. Don't be too positive or too negative until you have the full context. Don't get caught in hearing what you want to hear.

Dealing with a Former CEO Who Is Now a Board Chair or Director, and/or a Significant Shareholder

The shadow of your former CEO can make it hard for you to operate as CEO—or call the baby "ugly."

Again, in many cases, the former CEO understands this dynamic and accepts it. They will often raise it with you. If they don't, you must. This is an essential time to get together and ask: "When, *not if*, I want to change something you put in place or kill something that was your creation, how will we deal with *that discussion*?

A common scenario is making changes to the executive team. This is the former CEO's team and will likely be the first point when you need to have a discussion about seeing the world differently. You are trying to be respectful to the person who built what you now lead, and who was supportive of you getting the CEO role. But you still need to do the things that you know need to be done and make the changes that the business needs for the longer term.

In one CEO transition I advised on, the new CEO was announced in January with an official start date of June 1.

I pushed for a meeting between the outgoing CEO, the CEO elect, and the chair to discuss how the power and decisions would be transferred with the hope that it would head off any conflict early.

The meeting danced around the topic until we had 15 minutes left, and I raised it directly. "We need to talk about how authority is transferred over the coming months."

The outgoing CEO sharply responded: "Well, I am still CEO until May 31." Silence from the chair and the CEO elect.

So, I challenged the view. "Many people across the organization will already be looking at the CEO elect as the CEO now. He will be under pressure to start acting like it. We need a plan for what decisions will be needed between now and June 1, and agree who should make them."

Fortunately, the outgoing CEO softened. Leaving a CEO role is often quite an adjustment. We worked through the list of current projects and upcoming decisions, and were able to assign the most appropriate decision process to each. One of the benefits of being an external advisor is to help remove potential friction points.

The Business Context

On July 6, 1988, the Piper Alpha oil rig in the North Sea exploded. The accident was a result, in part, of failing to adequately check some of the established yet simple systems that had been operating faultlessly for over a decade. The scale of the blast was enormous, with flames shooting 90 meters (295 feet) in the air, visible up to 100 kilometers (62 miles) away. A total of 167 people died—the largest number killed in an offshore accident.

Hoping the fire would burn out or that emergency systems would soon control the fire, the initial response from the surviving workers was to lock themselves in a secure room. Eventually realizing this wouldn't work, three men made their way to the edge of the rig platform and were faced with two very tough choices: stay on the platform waiting for a rescue crew or for the emergency systems to kick in, or jump into one of the coldest and most hazardous oceans on the planet, where the risk of death by drowning or hypothermia was almost certain. Two leapt into the ocean and survived, albeit severely injured. Unfortunately, the other man chose to stay and died waiting for the rescue helicopters to arrive.

This is the origin of the commonly used business phrase "a burning platform," which explains a problem, issue, or threat that requires immediate action. Fortunately, most of the times it is used in corporate speak, lives are not at stake.

Burning platforms can give you something to focus on and hopefully solve. It focuses your attention on what you *should* be doing (among the many things you *could* be doing). It also offers the chance for you to become a savior, riding in on your white horse to kill the dragon. The caution is that burning platforms in business lexicon can be overused, and it may appear to some that you are *looking* for a dragon to slay. Be careful in using the term casually— remember that people will take what you say very seriously as CEO (including taking it home to the dinner table).

You can often find yourself in a Catch-22 situation: tackling the burning platform can stall many of the initiatives you will need for mid-term success, but your mid-term and long-term success are dependent on how you solve the immediate challenge. Move quickly and carefully. Successfully managing a CEO transition in a business that is on fire is quite an experience.

Turnaround

If you are at the helm of a business that requires immediate, significant, and substantial changes in order to survive, you'll be expected to make decisions much sooner than if you were at a company that was ticking along nicely. And you'll need to be comfortable making these decisions when you have limited context.

It is not uncommon for CEOs coming into a turnaround situation to accelerate wholesale senior leadership changes, dispose of businesses or business lines, contract geographically, or push ahead with mergers and acquisitions very early on.

This is the situation Mark Clouse encountered when he became Campbell's CEO. "I didn't come in and observe for 90 days, take stock of where we were, and then map out a plan. That just wasn't realistic with the situation we were facing." He continued, "You wait 90 days, and the business could be another 10 feet underwater."

Drawing on his time in the military, Mark had a clear idea of the immediate direction he wanted to take:

First, we had to shrink the battlefield. We had to stop fighting on so many fronts at the same time. We all know of at least one great army in history that lost because they were overextending themselves by fighting too many battles at the same time.

Next, I needed to make our focus super clear and super simple. There's another lesson from the military, which is that your mission should be so simple that if everyone on the battlefield were to die, except for the private, he or she would still know what to do. I'm happy to say that's not exactly the situation in the business world, but the principle is still helpful.

So, I chose to keep it simple. I knew that even if
I was only 70% right, we were still making progress
toward something and that is so important for an
organization that had gone through a very challeng-
ing stretch.

Continuation

Businesses that fit this category—with a solid foundation, efficient organizational structure, good levels of talent, and a stable record of growth—will often require their new CEO to broadly continue the existing strategy. There is always an opportunity for some realignment, but essentially the path is clear.

Before becoming Campbell's CEO, Mark Clouse helmed Pinnacle Foods, a role he took over from a loved and successful CEO. "The business was in great shape when I joined Pinnacle—a very different story from Campbell's situation," he said. "The big thing I did when I got to Pinnacle was to communicate that there wouldn't be any hard lefts or hard rights. I explained that I was not coming in as the new person to yank the steering wheel one way or the other. But what we were going to do was probably merge a little bit left or a little bit right, where we needed to make improvements or capitalize on opportunities."

This can be hard for incoming CEOs. Having nothing to fix does not play well into the psyche of many high-performing executives who have an underlying belief that they can do things very well, if not better than most.

Fortunately, there is no such thing as a perfect business, despite what you may have been told by the board, your predecessor, or even the market. As the new CEO, you are the steward of your organization and the way you see the world, or attribute value to opportunities, risks, and future trends will differ from others' views. You can make changes (hopefully positive), and you will over time get comfortable doing so.

The potential pitfall is that, in the spirit of "if it ain't broke, don't fix it," your organization may be more watchful for mistakes, and more sensitive to them, than in a turnaround situation. This is where the communication around your early decisions become critical (see Chapter 5).

Outsider or Insider

Your transition to CEO will be affected by the nature of whether you have been groomed and promoted internally, or found as part of a search process and joined from another organization or even industry.

If boards could have their cake and eat it too, they would argue that the best CEOs are those who are able to combine the traits of both insiders and outsiders—a CEO who could blend an insider's understanding of the organization, its culture, challenges, and opportunities with an outsider's objectivity and willingness to throw out things that are no longer working.

Neither transition is inherently easy. I would argue that although the challenges are different, it is not an automatic advantage to come from within. In fact, coming into the CEO role from outside can provide some distinct advantages, too.

Being the Outsider

One CEO I interviewed told me that becoming the CEO of a new organization is very much like the reality show

Storage Wars, "They pull up the shutter and you get a quick look, then you commit to buying the contents. It is not until after you have bought it that you get a really good look and work out what you have gotten yourself into."

For context, *Storage Wars* is a reality show in which bargain hunters and secondhand dealers bid on and buy discarded storage units in the hope of finding items of value. As part of the bidding process, the shutter of the storage unit is opened, but potential buyers can only look from outside. The shutter is then closed, the bidding begins, and the winner takes possession of the storage unit to find treasure, or junk.

This lack of understanding of the organization does not only increase your risk of making a mistake early on. It also slows your progress.

Having said that, externally recruited CEOs do enjoy certain benefits. They can ask the "dumb questions" of the business around why things are the way they are. Internal CEOs rarely have this luxury.

External hires also bring the benefit of an outside perspective. To quote Albert Einstein, we cannot solve our problems with the same thinking we used when we created them. This is often a consideration as to why an external CEO is appointed (as well as the fact that there is often no suitable succession candidate).

On the flipside, external CEOs can find it easier to make the tough decisions. As Lyssa McGowan at Pets at Home explained, one big benefit in coming from outside is that most organizations have decisions that probably should have been made, but were too hard to make for the incumbent CEO.

"If you have been in an organization for three, five, or ten years, then you are lapping your own decisions and actually making significant change is really, really hard."

As an outsider, you don't have the emotional or personal attachment to things that happened in the past. But you can't sit on your hands.

As Lyssa explained, "You need to make the changes early before *you* become emotionally attached to the way things are being done."

For Lyssa, this meant bringing her executive team together in her first week to cut the list of projects down from 60 to 20. She quoted Steve Jobs saying, "There's no such thing as a small project. Every project requires people and resource and governance. It might feel small, but the aggregation of lots of small things is to distract you from where the organization's going."

The challenge, of course, is you have to know the business well enough to know you're making the right decisions. The balancing act of acting quickly, doing the hard stuff, killing the sacred cows that need to be killed. It's tough to be sure.

Lyssa understands this challenge well, "You might be stepping on landmines, so you need to work hard to get people feeling comfortable enough to tell you when you are. But sometimes, you still need to go ahead and blow them up."

Being the Insider

Internally promoted CEOs certainly have an advantage in terms of business acumen and in understanding the culture. There's often a "golden period," when you know about the change, but the organization does not. This gives you the transparency and access at your old level, allowing you to ask questions without many of the restrictions of a CEO. If you have this opportunity, it is not one to waste.

This is where you can really get people's opinions on areas of the business and importantly what they would change or do if they could. Not quite the setup of the TV show *Undercover Boss*, but close.

You will be familiar with how the business operates, both above and below the line. Plus, you will have established relationships and the know-how to get things done (and how things really work). While you may be *au fait* with the issues in other functions, it's unlikely that you will have delved into them to the same breadth and depth as required to by a CEO, nor will you have the technical understanding to make informed decisions.

This can be a blind spot—as it was for one internally promoted CEO in the insurance industry. "I very quickly realized that there were so many more moving parts and barriers than I had seen, and I felt a little foolish, actually," he told me. "Most of the things I had planned to do straight away were just not possible. There were also trade-off issues for any decision that I wanted to make. At the start, I definitely felt at a bit of a loss."

It is natural to sit in your protected seat on the C-suite and make assessments about what you would do or would have done had you been CEO when X, Y, or Z happened, what I call the "when I rule the world trap."

Then you become CEO and soon realize that there are many more moving parts, complexities, influences, and variables. This can negatively affect your confidence, and if you hold onto the expectations you had before, you run the risk of making decisions or acting in ways that are less than ideal. The most common of which is stubbornly pushing ahead with initiatives that, in the light of day, are no longer right. Or ignoring or stifling inputs from your team, fueled by the belief that as the internal CEO you have thought this through and should have the right plan.

Marc Bitzer, who spent 18 years at Whirlpool before he became CEO, felt that knowing every corner of the business is "probably the biggest liability of insiders."

PepsiCo's Ramon Laguarta agreed, adding, "Being internal, you know the details and you have your developed intuition. But you have to be super patient. Listen, listen, and listen. You have to listen twice as much as you talk, more actually. If you don't, it could derail you because you think you know it all."

Another challenge an internally promoted CEO can face is that you are already known. That means you will be prejudged. People will have formed views on your strengths and your weaknesses. If you want to change the type of leader you are as CEO—or need to—you will have a much harder time doing so. The longer you have been with the organization, the stronger and deeper these views are.

And finally, one of the biggest disadvantages of being an internal hire is that once you're announced as the new CEO, you essentially start. Even if your predecessor is still in role, the power starts shifting to you almost immediately. People start lobbying you to get their projects through, particularly if they're on a long-time horizon, which can lead to an awkward period of double-hatting.

It often leaves little time to take a physical break before your official transition, when you can research, network, and get ready for the role. You may get to step away for a couple of weeks, but that's much less than an outside hire would typically take. And, as any proponent of transition success will tell you, preparation time is critical.

The New CEO Checklist

- **Set your plan.** A well-considered transition plan before you begin will have a significant impact on the success of your transition. It's a compass that will guide you (and the organization) forward during the uncertain early weeks and months.

- **Think back to front.** With so many competing priorities early on, it's often helpful to begin by thinking about your end goals. Look through the lens of legacy-building and what you want to be remembered for. Then work backward from there.

- **Bake in flexibility.** No plan is infallible, especially as new crises emerge at breakneck speed. Understand that you exist in the unconscious incompetent stage before you begin—and that you'll need to keep revisiting your plan, adjusting to events and new information that arises.

- **Don't have all the answers.** Your first few days and weeks as CEO will validate your thinking—and challenge it. Leave room to learn from your board members, your executive team, and other key stakeholders about your potential blind spots.

- **Remove the blinkers.** Your transition plan cannot exist in a vacuum. Take time to really assess the state of play that you'll find yourself in. Overlooking the influence of your predecessor, the organizational context, or your background will significantly undermine your early success.

PART II

Out of the Blocks: Making the Right Start

CHAPTER 3

Burst the CEO Bubble

"Nobody tells you the whole truth in the boardroom. There are two floors that are real: the factory floor and the trade floor. Everything in between is PowerPoint."

—Marc Bitzer, CEO, Whirlpool

One of the most common analogies CEOs use when describing the role is that it feels like you exist in a bubble—that you're surrounded by an invisible film that isolates you from what's really going on and what people really think and feel.

Or, as the well-known saying, adapted for the business world, goes, "As CEO, you can count on two things—you will never be given a cold coffee and you will never hear the whole truth."[1]

People *will* treat you differently now that you're CEO. You can think you are the same person as before, act the same, think and feel the same, but you are not the same. You are the CEO.

As CEO, your jokes will be funnier, and your stories will be more interesting. But you will also be further from the truth and challenged less.

For these reasons, you need to burst the bubble as soon as you can. And stop it reforming, which it can do multiple times during your tenure.

Ultimately, only you can burst the bubble. First, you have to acknowledge that you are in one. Then you have to work constantly to break it, or at least create some holes in it so you have the information you need to be effective (beware that, for some organizational cultures, the natural state is to keep moving the CEO back into the bubble).

Bursting the bubble involves adjusting your thinking and behaviors—to create an environment in which people feel comfortable telling you what they're really thinking *and* to remove your biases, so you open yourself to the true realities in front of you, rather than trying to confirm what you think you already know. In other words, the only way you burst the CEO Bubble is from the inside out.

* * *

See More, But Hear Less

I always smile when a CEO tells me that they have their finger on the pulse and know exactly what is happening across their organization.

Yes, you now have visibility over the entire business—no one can *see* as much as you can. The trade-off of that greater visibility is that you are as far from the frontline as you can get, and the number of layers between you and "them" has increased. So, while you are able to *see* more, you will *hear* less.

This paradox is harder to accept for CEOs who are promoted internally than those hired externally. When you join a new organization, your expectations regarding information are measured; you accept that people will not be as forthcoming until they get to know and trust you.

But when you have already spent significant time at an organization, you are accustomed to a certain level of information, both receiving and sharing, and expect it to stay the same when you're CEO. It does not. The members of your old team are now two levels from you, and they need to go through another person to get to you. The people below that are even further away.

Each of these layers will, to varying degrees, filter information. The same way the executive team manages the information going down the corporate hierarchy, people below you manage the information going up. If you don't believe this is happening to you, it is one of your blind spots.

There are many reasons people filter information. Sometimes, it's because they think you do not need to know. Often, it is out of fear, delaying bad news in the hope of solving it before they need to explain it.

As Walt Bettinger II, the CEO of Charles Schwab, described, people tell you what they think you want to hear and are fearful to tell you the things they believe you don't want to hear.[2]

But it's also true, PepsiCo's CEO Ramon Laguarta told me, that people want to make the CEO happy. "This doesn't happen as much when you are in an operational role, but when you're the CEO, people carefully position everything they tell you," he said. "I noticed almost immediately a different level of form versus substance. It means you need to be curious to ensure you learn what is really happening."

Even more common is that people want to look good in front of the CEO. Whirlpool's CEO Marc Bitzer found early on that his senior leaders were heavily rehearsing presentations before bringing them to him. "They prefilter," he said. "And I hate filtered coffee; I like espresso," he laughed.

Marc continued, "It's not that your leaders are lying to you, but the real picture of what's really going on, how the product is really leaving a factory and how they are really showing up on the trade floor is not necessarily what they are sharing with you."

"They're not consciously misleading you. But everybody wants to look good. There's a little bit *La Bella Figura* in all of us," he said (referring to the Italian expression of making a good impression).

Be Curious, Not Right

When you start your new role of CEO, you will be more successful if you focus on being curious instead of being right. (There will be plenty of time to be right later.)

Early on, learning should be your top priority. Some people will be more open and candid with you in your early days and weeks than later and so it pays to be highly inquisitive. Stay in this mode as long as you can (some, including me, would argue that being curious is something that you should maintain to your long-term benefit as a CEO).

Truly curious leaders are less prone to hubris and ego. They are willing to be challenged and are comfortable to be proven wrong, which not only makes them more open to the information available, but it makes people more willing to tell them what they're really thinking, feeling, or seeing, without fear of reprisal.

Curiosity is a wonderful trait and one that you see more in confident leaders who are not challenged by a personal insecurity about needing to be the smartest person in the room—all of the time.

One of the issues with curiosity is that it can wane as experience increases. As you get longer in the tooth, the weight of experience often starts to dampen your curiosity. This is why high levels of curiosity are often labeled as "childlike."

This is a risk that you'll need to mitigate.

At the more extreme end of the spectrum are CEOs who deliberately avoid curiosity. You may have the expectation of yourself that now you are CEO you need to have all the answers. But you were not selected as CEO because you are always right.

Of course, some people are more naturally curious than others, and you may find yourself in the camp where curiosity is not commonly associated with the *way you lead*. Don't let that get in the way. In every leadership transition, you get to refine some or all of your leadership style. Being curious is like being a better listener; it can be massively improved with attention, focus, and some self-regulation.

Keep in mind the quote from Maya Angelou, the American author, poet, and civil rights activist: "Do the best you can until you know better. Then when you know better, do better."

As the new CEO, there is much that you know, much that you don't know, plus a good amount that *you don't know that you don't know* (unconscious incompetence). You'll do best if you see this as an opportunity, rather than a challenge.

The benefits of staying in a learning mindset, of opening yourself up to challenge, are significant, as PepsiCo's Ramon Laguarta found. He focuses on making sure he creates a space for others to tell him what they really think. "It's one of the most important things you can do as CEO and is something I focus on every day."

He adopted this mindset even before becoming CEO, as he progressed during the selection process, and had time to reflect on the things that he wanted to do when he took the helm. "I thought the company had become too focused on margins, so I wanted us to pivot to growth," he said. "Secondly, I wanted to drive a big cultural shift to make the company more entrepreneurial and more transparent. And finally, I wanted to accelerate our digitalization and environmental transformation efforts."

Recognizing that this was only his view, he was keen to test his ideas. So, like Hans Vestberg, who is introduced in Chapter 2, he ran day-long sessions with people from across the company—the leadership team and those below it—where he asked for their thoughts, opinions, and co-creation on these areas.

For Ramon, it was a way to not only get their feedback and input, but also put a stake in the ground that the new culture of the company would be more bottom-up, and less top-down. "I had my vision for the company and I decided to empower this group to co-create the new strategy with me," he said. "I must tell you, I was quite surprised by how positively the process went and how it helped me."

There was an added, knock-on benefit as well: greater exposure to PepsiCo's U.S. team (the largest in the company), which Ramon, who'd spent most of his career in Europe, had more limited exposure to. "The personal relationships that I had built through the pre-work, not only with the U.S. team, but broadly around the company helped me significantly," he said. "It gave me a strong platform in the first year."

So, doing the pre-work pays dividends in the long run.

Two Ears, One Mouth

A clear aspect of curiosity (and an antidote to the challenge of not really knowing what is going on) is asking the right questions—and really listening. It's obvious, but easy to forget when you are moving fast in your early days as a new CEO. There is a Turkish proverb that says, "If speaking is silver, then listening is gold."

Meet plenty of employees during your transition and beyond. Embarking on listening tours, opening up the hierarchy, and asking them what the organization should be doing can broaden your sources of intelligence. People "at the coal face" know the operations and their part of the business intimately because they are in direct contact with customers, and are exposed to complaints and compliments. They also know where the processes and systems break down and how employees fix or work around them.

It's a powerful way of bursting out of the CEO Bubble—but an underused one. In RRA's research, 49% of CEOs said they spent too little time with middle managers and frontline employees.[3] But for those who do, it can be an invaluable way to get a feel for what's really going on.

For Whirlpool's CEO Marc Bitzer, it involved keeping Thursdays and Fridays clear in his calendar from Day One to visit the factories and stores—the parts of the organization that he believes he can get the truest sense check of what's going on.

For Carol Tomé, CEO at UPS, it meant asking her SLT to deliver packages to better understand the frontline experiences of its thousands of delivery workers. "Most had never done that before," she said. "I'm like, 'You're kidding!'"

For Starbucks CEO Laxman Narasimhan, it meant spending half a day each month working shifts at one of the coffee giant's outlets.[4]

For Uber's CEO Dara Khosrowshahi, it involved spending months during the pandemic driving the streets of San Francisco, either as a courier for its food delivery service or picking up passengers for its ride-hail business.[5]

And for Airbnb CEO Brian Chesky, it meant committing to living only in the company's network of rental properties.[6]

In some cases, employee perspectives can be a better predictor of downward trends than data in spreadsheets. Ask them what you can do to make their lives better, what gives them satisfaction, what drains their motivation, what needs to be preserved, and what is ripe for change. Listen with true empathy and compassion, rather than just seeking facts. Answer their questions honestly and manage their expectations.

If you can create an authentic engagement, you will potentially have the start of an invaluable information exchange that will help you make better decisions and build a better culture. Listening has an added benefit of smoothing the way when you are ready to set out your vision. As the saying goes, "Seek first to understand and then to be understood." Eventually, you will need people to understand what you want—you will spend much of your time as CEO ensuring your audience understands what you want to achieve and why. Your ability to do this will be super charged if you first *listened*.

Listening, But Not *Really* Listening

Many leaders believe they are better-than-average listeners. Unfortunately, many find out the hard way that this is not the case. There is a difference between a *willingness* to listen and an *ability* to listen. I often share the story of one CEO I worked with in order to get new clients to stop and reflect on whether they have this blind spot.

The CEO in question was keen to meet with the frontline and held a series of listening post meetings at various locations with mixed success. Like many CEOs, his mind ran at an almost unsustainable pace at times, and this was made worse due to being new in role and new to the organization.

At one location, where he had already been alerted to some performance issues, he met the manager of the operation and asked how she was. She told him she was trying to do her best, but it was her father's funeral the day before.

The CEO said, "Good," and launched into the first of many questions that he was burning to ask. He didn't notice his faux pas of completely ignoring her response to his question. But everyone else did. His lightbulb moment only happened when I completed the stakeholder feedback. He immediately took steps to correct his error, apologizing to the manager, and traveling back to the location to invest time in her and the team.

Ultimately, when you are new to a role, information and context are your key gaps. You have the capabilities and skills, but what you lack is the detail. The quicker you can learn, the quicker you will perform. But you will need to be careful that early interactions don't become a version of the Spanish Inquisition. You will have more questions than they do answers, and each answer spurs another line of questioning. The whole time your mind is racing to put it all together. For you, it's great, you are learning. For the others, it can be overwhelming. They can leave your early meetings feeling exhausted and anxious. Be clear from the start that you are here to understand, not to judge.

At the same time, be careful that, in your eagerness to learn, you do not inadvertently turn meetings into a performance review. For example, when someone tells you what they (or the organization) did, there is a big difference between you saying, "Why didn't you do x instead?" versus "What were the other options at the time?" followed by, "Why did you discount those?"

The first response is a performance appraisal—you went left, why didn't you go right? The second is a better line of questioning as it makes fewer assumptions and is less aggressive. Even if your intent is good and you are showing how eager you are to learn, it will still feel like a critique.

One of the assumptions that you want to be mindful of is the one that a decision was not "fit for purpose." Hindsight is a wonderful thing, so they say, and the rear window is always clearer that the front one.

However, when you are new to the CEO role, you need to be really careful not to come across as damning things that were done or decided in the past. There will likely be things that the organization or the individual regrets.

Acknowledge that fact and also that the intent at the time was not the issue.

Where they don't see it, but you do, try to understand the circumstances—was the decision a fair one at the time considering the available information and options? Was it fit for purpose at the time?

If so, then it is easy to acknowledge that it was the right decision at the time, and still make the assessment that it is no longer working and needs changing. This is acceptable. What is less acceptable is a new CEO condemning something without the context and understanding, or without acknowledging that the people involved might not have had all the context and understanding needed.

Consider this phrasing that I helped a CEO with, who had entered a business with a shopping list of issues. "I can see why we chose this CRM system five years ago: at the time it was the best choice for the business, and had I been here, I would have likely made the same decision. However, as we have grown, changed, and shifted, it is clearly not the right system for us now and we need to get moving on changing it." This is quite different to what he really wanted to say, which was some version of, "Why on earth are we using this CRM system; you would have been hard pressed to find a worse one for this business unless your intent was to drive every single customer away."

Check Your Biases at the Door

Humans have biases. You have biases, probably more than you accept (this is known as egocentric bias, which is the tendency to see yourself as less biased than other people). If you are a senior executive, you will have likely been working with your biases and "on them" for a long time.

Working on understanding and mitigating your biases is a key aspect of leadership (and human) development. There will be several that will impact the way you think and operate, consciously and subconsciously. You should make this part of your ongoing accountability and growth, especially as CEO, as your biases now have a much greater chance of impacting a larger group of people.

One of the biases to be especially careful of in transition is confirmation bias—the tendency to look for or interpret information to support a prior view or belief. A common example occurs when leaders interpret the data in a way to justify their position on a particular topic. What do they say—that 78% of all statistics are made up on the spot?

As much as you try to go into the role fairly open-minded, you will be making judgments, decisions, and plans as soon as the CEO role is offered to you (longer if you are internal).

When you are new in your CEO role, your confirmation bias will be in overdrive. The time between being offered the CEO role and starting will be full of assumptions and assessments, some founded in legitimate data and others based on more intangible sources.

However, there is a more sinister aspect of confirmation bias in transition: it feels good. Finding things that you expected to find will feel great. Actually, it will feel fantastic. It will massively help your confidence to be right about a great number of things.

Why?

Because if your assumptions about the business and its people were correct, then the board has made the right decision—you *are* the right person for the role and you *can* do this.

This is a dopamine hit and a major blind spot.

I interviewed a chair, an ex-CEO himself, about his new CEO and the issue of confirmation bias early on. The chair said that the CEO needed to be careful that she does not just see and hear what she wants to see and hear.

In his experience, what you observe as first principles as a CEO are not entirely accurate because you are in the CEO Bubble.

You need to learn and to understand the business, not look for things that confirm what you thought going in. Adopt the approach of "inspect what you expect." Be extra critical of the things that you predicted, and of the things that make you feel good, smart, and completely qualified. Beware of feeling happy that you were right. Ask yourself questions like "Where is the truth in this?" and "What needs to be true for this assumption to be correct?"

Marc Bitzer, whom we already met, was well aware of the risk of confirmation biases when becoming CEO of Whirlpool, where he'd already spent 18 years in multiple leadership roles. "There is a gravity that pulls on every successful manager, an incredible instinct toward telling people how to fix particular business issues. This gravity was a challenge because I knew every corner of this company."

For Marc, one of the biggest learnings was ensuring his biases didn't bleed into how he led his executive committee. "Ultimately, if all you do is give orders, all you get are order takers." He continued. "If you become CEO from inside, it is because you delivered, you delivered results, you delivered performance, you delivered impact and largely it came because you knew how to pull the levers etcetera. But now you have an executive committee: 10 other people who are equally successful and driven, and who don't want to be told what to do every day."

Marc moved into understanding that he will never have an accountable management team if he doesn't divest control. And, that there is actually an added benefit to his own success in doing so. "The danger is that the organization falls into this habit of Marc said X and Marc said Y. It is easy for many things that are done and decided in the organization to be labeled as something 'Marc said,' whether it is true or not. I need to be very careful."

He added, "Sometimes I joke with people that I don't even have enough time in a day to have said everything that people claim I have."

Avoiding this situation starts with being self-aware of the risk, like Marc was. But the Whirlpool CEO went a step further, pushing his SLT (and himself) to adopt an outside-in perspective.

He asked the team to think about what it would be doing differently if it was, for example, bought by a private equity firm or attacked by an activist investor. "Let's play devil's advocate," he told them. "What would somebody else do just to challenge our own thinking?"

Marc also encouraged his team to tell him when he is wrong. "Early on, they would email occasionally to call me out. You can't underestimate the importance of this. Because you're never going to be 100% right."

The New CEO Checklist

- **Accept that your relationships will be different now that you're CEO.** If you are humble, this will take longer for you to embrace than for others. But you do need to accept it. It is unfortunate, but it is the reality. Don't be offended, don't take it personally. It is part of the job.

- **Burst the "CEO Bubble" as quickly and as often as possible.** Work hard to ensure that you get the information you need to be effective and adjust your thinking, so you don't perpetuate the challenge. The sooner you burst the bubble, the quicker you will begin to perform well as a new CEO.

- **Find your espresso machine.** The debate and healthy discourse that you enjoyed as a C-suite leader or regional leader no longer exist. If you are lucky, you will have a couple of people who are comfortable to tell you the truth. If you do, keep them close; they are extremely rare and valuable.

- **Listen more than you talk.** Stay in learning mode throughout your transition. Set the stage for people to tell you what they really think and open up your ideas (and yourself) to constructive challenge. You were given two ears and one mouth for a reason.

- **Beware of your unconscious incompetence.** There will be a lot you don't know yet as the new CEO. Don't let confidence, biases, or ego get in the way of seeing the true picture in front of you. Make a list of assumptions prior to starting—and keep stress testing them as new information becomes available.

CHAPTER 4

Act Discerningly

"There is a time to let things happen, and a time to make things happen."

—Anonymous

The hardest part of a CEO transition is finding the right balance between listening and learning versus acting. How fast is too fast? How slow is too slow?

Do you come in and take immediate action to make things better and have an impact? Or do you keep your powder dry while you move around the organization listening, engaging, and learning?

I have had these conversations with every CEO I have worked with, and often several times over and again.

Should I take my time and learn the organization?
Yes.
But if I move too slowly, do I run the risk of the board getting rid of me?
Yes.

Do people need to feel the impact of a new CEO?
Yes.
But do I run the risk of losing people because I
move too fast?
Yes.
So, what should I do—be patient or go fast?
. . . Yes!

The hard truth is that it is impossible to answer the final question definitively. There is no answer that is always right, all of the time. Unfortunately, the CEO role is full of paradoxes, contradictions, and judgment calls—especially when you're in transition.

The decision about how fast to go—and what to focus on—will be heavily influenced by the organizational context you face (see Chapter 2). Sometimes the situation will dictate that you can't wait—for example, in the context of a turnaround or when joining an organization in crisis. In other scenarios, it will pay to slow down or scale back your actions.

But from my privileged position of sitting alongside CEOs in transition (and not being them), it is easy to answer the question about how fast to move. The answer is, of course, that you should act as fast as you can, once you have learned what you need to learn in order to make good decisions.

There are some general principles that can help you navigate this complex and high-stakes balancing act in your CEO journey. Not all will apply to you, but they should help you understand the scenarios when you can slow down, while still showcasing your intentions as a new CEO—and situations where you have no choice but to go big or go home.

Rethink the First 100 Days' Mindset

When there is a new president, national leader, and, yes, CEO, there is intense focus on their first 100 days: what they plan to do versus what they actually do.

As CEO, you will face no shortage of people telling you to do things as fast as possible at the start. But frequently I see that the greatest source of pressure often comes from within. *You* will want to move quickly, deliver, and achieve. This is common. As is explored in Chapter 3, you will want to prove to the business, to the market, and most importantly to yourself, that you are the right choice and up to the task—not in over your head.

You will likely have spent time before becoming CEO thinking about the early actions you plan to take. It will be a regular point of discussion around your transition and in everything you read. You'll have undoubtedly been told that your early actions (or wins) will set the scene for your tenure. While this might be true, the thing to remember is that *early* does not mean *immediately*.

Unless you're in a serious turnaround situation or in crisis management mode, the opportunistic focus on your first 90 or 100 days is overstated. The complexity of the CEO role, coupled with the nuances across the organization and its culture, means that it will take longer to get comfortable in the CEO role than any other you have experienced. There are simply more moving parts, and dramatically more responsibility, scope, and attention.

At the 100-day mark, you will still be finding your feet, let alone nailing it. Your ability to have significant impact by this point is low.

You will also still lack a lot of context, knowledge, experience, and information (at varying levels). This is applicable whether you are external or internal, although it is much more prevalent when you are external. So if you move too quickly toward the psychological 100-day deadline, the risk of making mistakes, or the wrong judgment call, is high.

If you need one rule of thumb, it would be to heed the lesson I often tell my clients: *if it is on fire, fix it. If it is smoldering, leave it alone until you have more context.* And remember, communication is your friend early on. Share your intentions and what you are doing—it helps significantly.

Festina Lente (Make Haste Slowly)

There is value in the concept of "going slow to go fast" *Going slow* means taking the time and making the effort to learn as much as possible before you act. The longer you stay in a learning state, the more information you will have to come out of the gates at the right pace, while also avoiding the risk of doing things that you later have to walk back or unwind.

One example of a CEO who took appropriate action to learn was a first-time retail CEO whom I advised. She'd spent her whole career in the retail sector, yet within two weeks of starting her transition, she still made the effort to work day and night shifts in the stores fronting customers. She did this for four weeks across multiple locations. "That is the heart of our business—everything else we do just supports that part," she told me. "If you want to understand your organization, you need to understand the frontline operations."

The senior ranks were a little shocked, but the wider organization loved it. Interestingly, when she made the first changes to her executive team and the management level below, most of the people she changed out did not share her view of how important it was to understand what's going on at the frontline.

Your learning curve in the first months of your role will be extremely steep. The expression "drinking from the fire hose" is a common way to describe your early weeks and months. What you understand at two weeks will more than double by the time you get to four weeks. What you know at four weeks will more than double by the time you get to the eight-week mark. And so on. Yes, the learning curve flattens out, but the point to remember is that, in transition, waiting another two weeks can make an enormous difference.

Ideally, you should resist making really big decisions or wide-sweeping changes early on (unless it's something on fire).

One internally promoted CEO I worked with had decided before officially starting that she would announce her new team structure after the first two weeks in her role. Moving fast on your team is generally a good idea (as we discuss in Chapter 7). But two weeks is, by any measure, at the extreme end of the spectrum. Not to mention that in her first two weeks significant gaps started to emerge in her understanding. I pushed hard for her to reconsider and wait.

I asked her, "Can we revisit your idea that it's important to announce the team structure in the first two weeks? Where did that come from?"

"I want to establish that I am here to drive change and I want people to know I'm ready to make the hard decisions," she replied.

"Hard decisions—yes. Bad decisions—no," I said. "What do you lose waiting another two weeks? No one has an expectation that this decision will be made this fast, except you."

She waited and then decided to make staggered changes over the next six months. In doing so, she avoided the very real risk of committing to a decision, and then having to fall on her sword and revert it later.

Often, it can help to document your early thoughts and recommendations, but stop short of actioning them until you have enough context.

* * *

Easy Wins

While you need to resist the pressure (internal or otherwise) to come in and fix or change everything straightaway, you will still want to make *some* moves during your transition, not least to signal your intentions as a new leader.

One mistake many new CEOs make is trying to "boil the ocean" in terms of their early actions. This is a great aspiration, but rarely can you achieve something really significant in your first weeks and months.

It's a lesson that RRA's former CEO Clarke Murphy learned quickly when he took on the role. "I tried to launch too many initiatives simultaneously. Everyone says don't do too much at once. You think you know better—you don't."

In the award-winning eponymous Apple series, Ted Lasso turns to a suggestion box to field ideas on where to focus his attention. If you have seen the show, you will know that many of the suggestions are unhelpful to say the least. In the end, Ted focuses on fixing the water pressure in the team showers. It's a humorous example of a very effective early action—something small, basic, and previously ignored, yet something that sends a clear message.

I'm obviously not advocating you bring out your own suggestion box. Instead, as you think through what you want to achieve early on, the ideas here will hopefully provide some direction. Remember, how your actions are perceived—whether just a convenient opportunity or a strategic win—will be up to how you explain it (see Chapter 5).

You will likely find a number of issues within the business that fall into the "early wins" category—problems that are small and easy for you as the new CEO to fix, to the thunderous applause of the crowd. Perhaps not quite. But keeping an eye out for wins like these is a great way to demonstrate positive intent early.

A CEO I helped transition effectively, for example, had joined an organization that had two locations in the head office city, literally across the street from each other. People in most divisions were spread across both buildings, driven by poor planning, laziness, and personal agenda around offices and views.

Each day, people could be seen going from one building to the other for meetings. Some floated between the two buildings so much that no one really knew where they were. Almost everyone moaned about how stupid it was.

Three weeks in, the CEO had heard enough, and by his fourth week, he made a decision about who should be sitting where. That weekend he had movers come in and put people in their new spots. One comment from the stake-holder feedback was, "The senior leadership have been saying it is too hard for two years and he fixed it in a month."

This action delivered several positive outcomes: it stopped a large amount of the negative noise in the business; it removed one of the excuses for lack of collaboration and teamwork; it improved efficiencies and office attendance; and it showed employees that they were important and high on the CEO's radar. It meant that the CEO started on a foundation of engagement and trust, which made it easier for him to push through more radical changes later on. We knew this because people continued to reference the office move as a reason to trust him.

It often makes best sense to find something that your employees, SLT, or board think is a small win, rather than seeking a significant problem to hang your hat on as CEO. Commonly, these are easy-to-address issues that can make a positive impact: fix IT or pay issues; fix physical office frustrations; or reduce or remove unnecessary reports; and so on.

Of course, these "easy wins" are not always present, so my advice is to take them when you can. But don't just mindlessly chase any win you can claim. Your earliest actions as CEO will send a clear message of what is important to you—it could be aimed at the team, it could be aimed at the shareholders, it could be aimed at the market, or it could be aimed at the board. Whichever direction you choose to go in sends a clear signal about your priorities. A good question to ask yourself when looking for a quick win, or acting upon it, is: A win for whom?

In many situations, it is beneficial to make your people feel first and foremost that they're the priority. This is what Ted did by fixing the water pressure.

Common Pain Points

Addressing a constant moan or common pain point is another good approach. This is what Stephanie Tully, CEO of Jetstar, did when she worked fast to change a key facet of the employee experience. Shortly after arriving, she went on a listening tour across Jetstar, meeting with its 7,000 people across the Asia-Pacific—not only to understand what was working and what wasn't, but to show that she "wasn't just going to run this business from an office in the city." To build trust.

"Within the first couple of months, I spoke with pilots, cabin crew, engineers, and airport staff, getting to know everyone and trying to understand the lay of the land."

She continued, "Everyone was telling me that they hated the uniform—that it was uncomfortable, that it had been 20 years and it had never changed. So, I said, 'Let's change it.'"

Straightaway, Stephanie kicked off a project to change the uniform. A new version, with a refreshed look and feel, will launch in 2024. The uniforms are better quality so will be longer lasting, making them more sustainable and ultimately cheaper too, and in the words of Stephanie, "everyone loves them."

"It's a symbolic act—it shows that you care, that you are listening, and you're willing to fight for things," she told me. "That's how you can get people on board with the changes that are needed. It has a contagious effect because it makes your leaders realize that they perhaps weren't listening enough before—that it probably shouldn't be me that's finding out these problems. It should be everyone as part of a system that is constantly looking to fix things and to improve."

One of the easiest things to do when you're going through your initial one-on-ones is to try and identify the common moan or pain point among the team. In my experience, you'll often hear a range of things, some small, some large. If you are able to solve one of the smaller ones quickly, it will go a long way to winning over your team—and often the wider organization.

Again, they don't have to be enormous, but they should be deliberate.

Early Moves

At a slightly larger scale than easy wins are a CEO's early moves—the more substantial decisions that are made during the transition period.

Often the early moves are things that the business is aware of already. It is rarely something out of left field that you suddenly discover. It is commonly a decision that the business has been struggling with for some time or an issue that just won't seem to go away. Different from easy wins (although it is all semantics), early moves change the business direction in some way or signal a future change.

Another new CEO I advised decided at around six months to sell a large underperforming area of the business. In his words, "Everyone from the board to the janitor told me that it was a dog, and it should have been sold years ago. When I asked why it hadn't been I got a variety of excuses and cop-outs. There was even a buyer for it. So, I did one last series of meetings asking for objections and for anything that I didn't know about it—nothing. So, I sold it and the transaction was completed in 60 days."

You will likely hear reference to the need for CEOs to make bold moves, especially in turnaround situations. (We discussed earlier that the business situation does affect how you approach your transition.) However, I do make the distinction here between early moves while in transition (your first 12–18 months—the focus of this book) and larger bold moves made later.

Research by McKinsey on the bigger moves and decisions made by more than 600 CEOs by the end of their second year found that the most popular, in order, were: management reshuffles; mergers or acquisitions; cost reduction programs; new business/product launch; geographic expansion; organizational redesign; business/product closure; strategic review and geographic contraction.[1]

Deal with the Messes

It is not uncommon to arrive as a new CEO and be saddled with problems that have existed for a long period of time, or to find that problems are sitting on your desk waiting for you. An example is entering an organization that is in the legal crosshairs. You have no choice but to deal with this— even if it wasn't part of your plan.

This can be a source of frustration and distraction for a new CEO. You start the role with the intention of learning the business, meeting key people, and addressing teams, but instead, you end up dealing with problems that should have been dealt with long ago.

One CEO, who inherited an organization with some deep-seated issues around culture and people, found herself dealing with three large legal cases as her first action

(continued)

as CEO. It took five months to settle them. The process was so encompassing that the CEO was essentially absent for the first couple of months, unable to enact many of the things that she had wanted.

At first, the broader organization misunderstood her focus. It wasn't until after two of the particularly sensitive cases were settled that she was able to let people know what she had been doing and why.

One of the cases was especially sensitive, due to the professional and personal impact it would have on the previous CEO and several large equity holders. The business had already spent tens of millions of dollars defending it, but it was clear it was unwinnable. The new CEO brought the parties together, confirmed that it would not be a positive outcome for the firm, and settled. The individuals involved were furious, but the business was ecstatic.

"We should have never been in that legal position, and it was pride and self-interest that kept us there," one leader said during stakeholder feedback. "She did exactly the right thing to settle it and to do it so fast was fantastic."

Still, it was not the start she had planned for, and going in, she did not have a full understanding of how severe the organization's external challenges really were.

Be prepared that some of your early focus will be lost to aspects like these. Allow some space in your planning. If you find that this is the case, then try to deal with them as fast as you can. Many are legal or contractual, and carry substantive potential impacts for the business. There will be many factors as to why they have not been settled before, none of which will really matter. The best thing for you and for the organization is that you clean them up as expediently as possible.

Clearing the Decks

There are some opportunistic benefits and advantages to being the new CEO. One of these is the lack of complete ownership of the current problems and financials in the business. Essentially, this is the process of clearing the decks, burying the dead, or kitchen sinking.

This lack of full accountability affords you, potentially, the unique freedom to make some financially unpleasant decisions. You will often see new CEOs identify the areas of the business that are not performing, or identify hard, but necessary decisions that will have significant financial impact, and address them very early—usually before their first full financial year.

Write-offs, write-downs, jettisoning poor-performing businesses, exiting poor-performing mergers or joint ventures, closing businesses/markets, changing supplier or employment terms or even making significant redundancies are all examples of a financial clearing of the decks that CEOs have made in order to set up the business, and their tenure, for success.

Where this opportunity presents itself, bring forward the financial pain and clear the decks for you and your team. Having a great first full financial year earns you the right for a second year. This is when you can really make a difference.

One CEO who inherited an outdated operating system with significant technical debt decided to contract and pay upfront for the replacement system before the start of her first full financial year. The business had been putting off this significant investment for several years, primarily because the outgoing CEO, who retired, knew that he would not reap the benefit of the new system, only the cost and pain of the change. While this is not good stewardship, it is a reality of human behavior, even, and often especially, at the CEO level.

In certain situations, the changes needed are obvious to the organization before you start. Where they are agreeable, there is an option for the outgoing CEO to clear the decks before they leave. It might also be possible for this to be managed by the CHRO or the chair. If it is a clear decision and the timing permits, then getting some of these done prior to you officially taking the role stops it from being something *you did* and can help you and your transition.

In another example, a new incoming CEO (whom I did not support) joined an organization where the average tenure of the leaders exceeded 22 years. He felt that the business needed a significant restructure to be in a position to compete over the next decade, but much of the processes and structure was tied to a 40-year-old operating and organizational model.

In the six months prior to his official start date, the chair, interim CEO, and CHRO made every leader three levels below the CEO redundant and invited them to reapply for their roles in the new organizational structure.

This cleared the decks for the incoming CEO and partially protected him from the negative blowback of this decision, which completely stalled the momentum of the business for three months. However, he managed to swiftly deal with a legacy leadership culture that could not take the business forward or through the change it desperately required. In his first financial year (partial year due to when he started), he had a nonrecurring expense due to the redundancies of close to $40 million, which at the time, was significant. However, he and his new team had a clean slate for change and performance in his/their first full financial year.

Think about the things that will force the business, and in turn, you to struggle over the coming year(s). Where you can, be bold and make the hard decisions. What is important for you as CEO is the business performance and outcomes. To be able to deliver on this you need to still be the CEO.

The New CEO Checklist

- **Adopt new metrics for your early success.** In many situations, the first 100 days is an artificial milestone. I prefer a different scorecard—one that looks at whether you have been respectful of what is in place, taken the time to understand the people and the culture, and made an undeniable effort to establish relationships with a multitude of stakeholders.

- **Go slow to go fast.** Unless you're in a turnaround situation or crisis, it pays dividends to not listen to the voices telling you to make changes immediately. Often, by slowing down at the beginning and taking the time to truly understand the context, you'll be able to accelerate faster later on.

- **Don't boil the ocean.** It's tempting to aim to deliver as much as possible in your early weeks. While your early actions in transition are important, they don't

(continued)

have to be enormous. They do, however, need to be deliberate.

- **Look for easy wins.** Look for the early actions that you can take to make your intentions as CEO clear—whether that's fixing a quick problem or addressing a common pain point. These can go a long way to showcase what you stand for and signal your priorities as the organization's new leader.

- **Fight the fires.** Naturally, there will be some issues that can't wait and that need addressing immediately. This is most evident in a turnaround situation, but it may also refer to making tough decisions relating to the finances or reputation. If it's on fire, you have no choice but to fix it.

- **Remember you don't always own it all upfront.** In the eyes of the market, you will not have full responsibility of the financial results until your first full financial year cycle. Take the opportunities this presents to clear the decks and solve long-standing or pressing issues early on—or even before you arrive. People understand that there are historical aspects that will govern your business' results in your first year. This works both positively and negatively. If the results are poor or even bad, they are not your responsibility, but there will be a big expectation that you fix them quickly. If they are exceptionally good, they are also not your responsibility and fairly or unfairly you will be expected to improve them regardless (maintaining is a distant second prize). Tough, I know.

CHAPTER 5

Get the Messaging Right

"A CEO's casual utterances can quickly become concrete buildings."

—Ron Williams, former CEO, Aetna

When Satya Nadella began at Microsoft as a young graduate in 1992, he reportedly told himself, "This is the greatest job on Earth. I don't need anything more."[1]

Little did this recently qualified engineer know that just 22 years later he would become the third CEO of one of the most powerful tech companies on the planet.

As he stepped into the CEO shoes in February 2014, it was not just a defining moment for Satya, but also Microsoft. There was widespread hope that Satya could help administer a shot in the arm for Microsoft, at a time when it was facing fierce competition on all sides. He vowed to accelerate the company's ability to bring innovative products to market faster, but in the eyes of some, it was seen as an Everest-scale challenge.

To say the world was watching for Satya's first move was an understatement—and he wasted no time in delivering. Just hours into taking the CEO seat, he emailed every one of the tech giants 128,000 employees with a note that was as humble as it was galvanizing. In just a little over 1,000 words, he unflinchingly set out who he was, why he was there, and what the company would do next.[2]

He painted an intimate picture of himself as a family man, who has a thirst for learning, and like everyone else, his own foibles. "I buy more books than I can finish," he wrote. "I sign up for more online courses than I can complete. I fundamentally believe that if you are not learning new things, you stop doing great and useful things."

He positioned himself as a collaborator-in-chief, letting it be known that he'd asked Microsoft founder Bill Gates to "devote additional time to the company, focused on technology and products," and crediting Qi Lu, then one of Microsoft's most celebrated computer engineers, for recently articulating that Microsoft's unique role in the world was to empower people to "do more."

Most of all, he brought the entire organization on the journey ahead. Across his email, he used the word *we* much more than *I*. This was not a letter about him. It was a new vision for every one of Microsoft's employees. "Many companies aspire to change the world," he wrote. "But very few have all the elements required: talent, resources, and perseverance. Microsoft has proven that it has all three in abundance. And as the new CEO, I can't ask for a better foundation. Let's build on this foundation together."

If anyone needed a master class on what to say as a new CEO, it was this. (It's perhaps one reason why this letter has been shared hundreds of thousands of times across the internet.)

What Satya did perfectly, from the get-go, was to own his narrative. He didn't wait for the business or market to do it for him. And even though news of his appointment had spread like wildfire across the media, he didn't assume that every one of Microsoft's employees had received the memo.

As Satya recently told *Fortune,* "However smart you are, if you come in and create more confusion at an already uncertain time, that's not leadership."[3]

A key part of your initial communication needs to be about you, why you're happy to be here and what you're going to do over the coming weeks and months. This is a critical juncture for your organization. And if you don't set the narrative, someone else will.

* * *

Being in a new CEO role is akin to a politician making a public statement—every day. While Satya nailed the first-day memo, it's just one of many early interactions that you'll need to get right. And as you may know by now, there's little room for error.

Everything you say and do is heavily scrutinized when you are the new CEO, unfairly so. Some describe it as feeling like you are constantly being filmed, with every action and word recorded. Taking a manager out for coffee, the inflection of your voice, things that you say you like or do not like all carry enormous weight, especially early on. People will latch on to everything. You may have been well-known previously, but now you're the main attraction. For some, this can feel overwhelming.

There's another side of this challenge, which Ron Williams, the former CEO of Aetna, described well. "The other thing you need to do is pay attention—100% of the time," he said. "I know that sounds like an impossible task, and it probably is.

But if you say 'yes' in a casual conversation, nothing happens. If you are the CEO, and you lapse for 15 seconds, next thing you know you have approved expenditure of $20 million."

He added, "You may not even be cognizant that's what you just did. So paying attention is one of the most critically important things you can do. Otherwise, it will come back to haunt you."

In my work with CEOs, I see time and again how communication missteps in their early days can linger and haunt the rest of their tenure. You may find (like many before you) that you need to work hard to make amends for comments or actions you made in your first few weeks and months that triggered a negative or hostile response.

One way to mitigate this is to "prep like a politician." It's good to have an almost political-like series of responses to the many questions you will get asked about your opinion and views. If you do not, it is likely you will get caught out. You are someone who has an opinion and are used to giving it. When pushed without a "go-to" response, you might end up saying more than you want.

Before you start, you'll want to prepare your narrative for the business and the market. Even though there may have been numerous media releases about your appointment, do not assume that everyone in the organization understands why you were selected and what your mandate is.

Being clear on your early messaging is vital. Many of the people I have advised have initially resisted this, saying that they've always been good on their feet, or they know what they want to say, or that they don't want a script as it will make it inauthentic. They are also often naïve about the amount of grace they will have, believing that people will be quick to forget. "I'm sure I won't say anything too bad, and if I do people will forgive me for being new."

No, they won't, and no they don't.

A "good on my feet" first-time CEO joined a turnaround situation in a very well-regarded brand, loved by many, but that had lost its way. He was the right person to take on the CEO role, having worked in the industry his entire career—he was ready for his new role.

Early in his transition, he ran an All-Hands meeting in the head office. He and I prepped for the session and as much as I encouraged him to plan his open and close, he was worried about sounding scripted and rehearsed. He wanted to ensure he was authentic. Confident in his ability to think on his feet, he went ahead knowing the key points. He invited me to attend, which I did.

He started well and spoke passionately about the rebrand. The audience was engaged and excited about the journey ahead. But as he got further into the presentation, he relaxed, too much.

He went past the point that he'd planned to stop at, and began to talk about people and culture—a tough topic for the business. He finished the presentation, with a nicer version of fit in or, well, move on: "So basically, if you feel it is going to be too hard, then this is probably not the place for you and you should make that decision now."

While this was a valid and an important message, this was not the appropriate forum, and it left the crowd suitably stunned.

He came up afterward and asked what I thought, to which I said, "Do you know what your closing statement was?" He was shocked and disappointed. He had certainly come across as authentic—he had told people exactly what he thought.

Fortunately, he took the time to reflect. And at the next event—an all-staff conference—he was disciplined not only about how he opened his presentation, but also how he ended it.

Another way to mitigate early communication mishaps is to have a communication plan as part of your transition planning. A good communication plan will cover your key messages and the medium of communications. It will give you clarity about what you will say, to whom, and how. (Communication is such a fundamental aspect of being CEO that beyond the transition period, many CEOs have a rolling communication plan to ensure that they are maximizing this aspect internally and externally.)

In Chapter 2, we met three-time CEO André Lacroix, who talked about the in-depth preparation and planning he adopts prior to his start date and for the first months. This includes his communication plan for how he will interact with everyone from his board, leadership team, and frontline employees to shareholders, investors, and the media.

"Your communication plan needs to be super sharp," he told me. "It's one thing to write your strategy, to have your operational plan, to set your goals, to analyze your risk and financial projection, but it's quite another to be able to extract the meaning of what you're trying to do in simple terms and explain it concisely to all stakeholders."

As part of his communication plan, André decides the three to five key messages that he wants to get across during his first 30 days—both externally and internally. (He is clear that you need to accept that what gets discussed internally also gets discussed externally and vice versa.)

Then, he moves onto the next 30 days, ensuring that no internal or external communication is made that doesn't align with his plan, particularly in the media. "There are very few leaders who can really improvise on the spot effectively, so the rest of us have to be very well prepared," he said.

Once the messages are set, it's then a question of making sure they're understood and absorbed. "As CEO, you need to repeat the key messages so often that you get tired of them," André told me.

Another CEO I interviewed joked that the CEO title should really be CRO—Chief Repeating Officer.

What to Say

When you are the new CEO, everyone is listening, almost hanging on your every word. Everything you say will be dissected, discussed, and retold at some level. You will be misquoted and misinterpreted. Be careful to not make promises that you might not be able to keep. Organizations and their people often have long memories. So, what should you say? These three phrases are fantastic during your transition, but they are also very powerful and applicable in your business-as-usual phase. Use them generously and often.

I Don't Know

Get comfortable saying "I don't know" because it's true and expected. At points during your transition, you will be

(continued)

asked for your view; people will rightly assume that you have one and will try to coax it out of you. However, this can be a trap or cause problems for you later. I advise CEOs to have a response ready along the lines of, "While I am starting to understand some of the key factors, at this stage, I don't think I have enough of an understanding to have a clear view."

How Can I Help?

When you are a new CEO, people will come to you with many problems, both current and historic. Be careful about making quick suggestions or deferring it back to the team member with, "You have a better understanding of what is going on, why don't you make the call." Ask instead, "How can I help?" Let them tell you what they need you to do and support them in that. It not only helps your team members, but also completely disarms anyone who is expecting you to come in and exert your power.

What Didn't I Ask, But Should Have?

You will have many meetings with employees, peers, and other stakeholders in which you will ask (hopefully) good questions. Most people will answer you diligently and honestly. But they may not go over and above without prompting. Asking, "What should I have asked about this but haven't?" will often generate a rich amount of extra information. "Oh, you should have asked about the first version of the project and why it didn't work," or "You should have asked why the manager before the last one was fired," or "You should have asked who the original sponsor was because then you would know that it was the chair."

Communication versus Action

The extent to which your transition is deemed successful early on will depend on your communication as much as, if not more than, your actions. Yet so many CEOs I work with over-index on the actions they want to take early on, and think much less about how to effectively communicate them.

It's understandable. As discussed in Chapter 4, being a high-achieving, high-performing executive, you'll no doubt feel the pressure to deliver quickly as CEO—to prove you are the right choice (to both the board and to yourself). It's natural to want to appease your internal dialogue about making an impact. But one of the paradoxes in transition is that you face this pressure to act at the exact moment when you lack the breadth of information you need to make the right judgment calls.

What you do have control over is *how* you choose to communicate—what you say to people about who you are; why you are there; what you are excited about; what you are learning, seeing, or hearing; what you are thinking about; and what you are planning.

The opportunity is to carefully plan your communication as much as you do your early actions and realize that you can, in some cases, achieve potentially more early on by communicating than acting.

Intent versus Behavior

You also need to be aware that there is often a discrepancy between your intent and your actions. Accept (at least in part) the quote from Stephen Covey, the author who reminded us that, "We judge ourselves by our intent, others judge us by our behavior."[4]

This is a reality for leaders at all levels across all organizations and transcends into our personal lives. Regardless of how pure our intent is in any given situation or action, if our behavior is interpreted differently, this is what will be remembered.

A good example is a CEO in a new organization who heard from many people that a particular well-established meeting was not very effective. So, before she had ever attended this meeting, she cancelled it. The intent was great: "Here is something that is wasting people's time and causing frustration, so I will stop it." However, her communication around the decision was left wanting.

Because she didn't communicate to anyone about why she made this decision and had never attended the meeting to verify her information, she considerably angered her team. They (rightly) took the view that the CEO didn't care enough to understand them or what they did.

This is one of the reasons why your behavior early in your transition is so important and why things that happen early on can stay with you, as a CEO for years. The hard truth is that at least one of your actions early on will be misinterpreted, whether you know about it or not.

One way to mitigate this is to be overt in communicating your intent early An example might be, "Thank you everyone for taking the time to attend this Town Hall. My intent in doing this is . . ." Or, "I have recently changed our meeting frequency and agendas, and my intent in doing so is . . ."

Checking your proposed course of action against your original intent can also help avoid issues. In doing so, you may find that there is a better course of action to achieve your desired outcome. You might hear, "If you really want that to happen, what works better here is . . ." If you do, it is a great sign.

Share a Collective Opinion, Not Your Own

As the new CEO, it's important to stay in learning mode early on—and talk about the fact that you're in learning mode often.

Being in a learning mode gives you an enormous benefit with your early communication: you don't have to state your views, and you can state what you are hearing and what you are learning.

The following phrases are deliberately in the present tense. Once you begin to say "This is what I have heard or this is what I have learned," it becomes fixed, locked, and committed. People will consciously and subconsciously hear your use of the past tense and their view will shift as a result.

- **What I am hearing is . . .** This is a great way to test people's reactions to an idea without owning it.
- **What people are telling me is . . .** This projects that you are sharing the ownership of ideas and approaches.
- **What I am learning is . . .** This gives you some wiggle room to test your understanding and gauge early reactions, and allows for people to feel comfortable to challenge you.

(continued)

- **My emerging understanding/thinking is . . .**
  Again, this offers you the chance of a litmus test, while also starting to answer people's questions about your strategy.

One CEO used this approach early on in her tenure to call out poor customer service. People were telling her that there was a problem, but no one wanted to own it. Around three weeks in, as part of a Town Hall meeting, she said, "Look I know that this is difficult, but I am hearing from a lot of you that our lack of customer service is at the center of why our organization is struggling. It used to be our USP, but over the last few years, it has fallen at an increasing rate. I am keen to get some thoughts in this forum." This opened the flood gates, and there were more comments than they could handle. The result was the elephant in the room was firmly on the table, and she could start to address it.

Another CEO used the approach to address a poor-performing executive team member saying, "I have been here a week and multiple people have told me that you are not a team player, throw people under the bus, and are only out for yourself. I felt I needed to raise this early. What are your thoughts?" Calling it out straightaway, before there was enough time for it to be the CEO's opinion, was the perfect way to have a conversation that resulted in an early resignation of someone who almost all the organization felt was not a culture carrier.

As you progress through your transition and your thinking becomes more concrete, you can change the tense to start saying, "Here is what I have heard." This signals that you have gathered enough data to have partially or fully formed a view.

Chicken Noodle Soup and Blue Walls

How you show up as a leader will shape the organization's set of accepted behaviors and norms. Everything you do is role-modeling—so be very deliberate and conscious here. You need to get used to the microscope of being CEO and learn how to best harness the attention to create a consistent, positive impact.

Everything you do sends a message. There is no such thing as noncommunication once you are CEO. There is nothing that "doesn't really matter" or "was not really important." If you say something to one person, you must assume you are saying it to everyone. You cannot make any other assumption here (the same rule applies with the media).

You should also assume that it will be retold in a number of different versions, altered, exaggerated, or downplayed, and given a different context. Do not be shocked when something comes back to you as something you said "verbatim" only for it to not resemble what you said at all. The same obviously applies to written communication. You should have some level of safety with your executive team and with the board, but you still need to be careful, and you need to be especially careful with the broader organization and market.

One first-time CEO in hospitality whom I advised was eager to get an understanding of the business, so one of her first moves was to make dozens of site visits. At each, she had a general structure of meeting with the team and managers, touring the venue, and holding an open "listening post" session. She was careful with her scripting, avoiding any judgmental language, asked good questions, and was very engaging.

During one of these site visits, she walked into a venue, where one wall was painted blue, a color that was not in the brand guidelines for the business. "That's a nice blue," she said, before moving on.

Two days later at another site visit she realized that the comment had been shared among the store managers and that the venue she was now visiting was making arrangements to paint a wall the same shade of blue.

They had heard she liked it and wanted to get it done before she had arrived, but had struggled to identify the right shade. She was surprised that such a small unintended comment had created such a series of actions, all in the attempt to impress the new CEO.

Another example of why it's important to be careful about what you say happened to a CEO who had just been promoted into the role. For him, it was a great lesson in not underestimating the importance of what you say to anyone in the organization.

One morning, after getting in early, he went into the cafeteria and started casually talking to the team. During the conversation, he asked what the soup of the day was.

"Chicken noodle soup," the cafeteria employee told him.

"Oh, I love chicken noodle soup," he said, heading to his office.

Around three months later, one of his assistants came into his office and somewhat awkwardly said, "Listen, I have had a ton of requests for you to go to the cafeteria and tell the staff that you like another type of soup than chicken noodle—they have served it every day since you told them that you loved it, and people are sick of eating it."

He managed to make a light-hearted moment out of it and went to the cafeteria to address the recent glut of chicken noodle soup. More beneficial, though, was that he was able to use it as an example of how the business needed to challenge what he says in order to make great decisions and drive successful outcomes. Anytime there is excessive nodding of heads in a meeting he asks, "Is this another chicken noodle soup moment?"

Once you become CEO, concepts such as privacy and "off the record" are a thing of the past. Every action you make and word you say will be subject to discussion and interpretation—big things and small ones: when you arrive for work, how you relate to people in formal and informal situations, how you prepare for meetings, how you allocate your time all matter. The old adage of "do as I say, not as I do" is now dead for you. Accept that people will do as you do, talk as you talk, and act as you act.

Nowhere is this more important than when it comes to navigating your own work-life balance. One CEO I worked with in the United States was genuinely committed to the health and well-being of the people in her organization. She focused heavily on ensuring that employees, and especially leaders, had the confidence to attend to their family commitments and treat them as importantly as their work commitments. She spoke about it at most meetings and praised people who took time off for their family. This was something she was truly passionate about.

The challenge came from the behavior she role-modeled. Her personal situation was such that she had the freedom to work at varying hours and for long periods. So people saw her as a "first in, last to leave" type of CEO and someone who would respond to emails at all hours, often immediately and even when on holiday.

When I did the stakeholder feedback, I heard that her observed work habits were having the greatest negative impact on women leaders who saw the CEO as a role model, and were questioning their ability to match her working hours and style. They were starting to doubt how realistic it was for them to aspire to be CEO.

This was devastating to the CEO. The thought that she was discouraging women leaders was more than upsetting. My discussion with her uncovered that she actually had a really clever way of scheduling her time and was meeting almost all of the personal commitments that were important to her, including good amounts of downtime when on leave. She felt that she had a great work-life balance, and I actually had to agree with her. The problem was that no one saw that and they certainly didn't believe it.

The solution was to start talking more openly about the time she was taking away from work to do personal activities, explaining how she managed her workload around these events, and being more transparent with her calendar. Instead of having "private" appointments, she labeled some of them for what they were: for example attending her daughter's college meetings, and so on. She also told her executive assistant to be open with internal people when they asked for time that clashed with a personal appointment. Instead of, "Sorry, she can't attend at that time," the person would be told, "Sorry, she is having an early dinner with her family that night and can't attend."

So, be intentional about how you're showing up. And recognize that, as CEO, you are ultimately responsible for projecting the right behaviors.

This nearly tripped up another CEO I advised early on in his transition. Like many CEOs, he put in long hours, working weekends and traveling frequently—and that meant he often sent emails outside work hours.

I raised it as a consideration early and his view was that his emails were mostly sent to the executive team members, who understood that they didn't need to respond immediately. Plus, "they also work weekends."

It came up again in his stakeholder feedback, when many of the executive team highlighted that their team members were feeling the pressure of the weekend emails.

We talked about it again, and his view remained that people understood that he worked weird hours and that he is sending emails when convenient to him, with no expectation of an "out of hours reply."

I pushed again, asking him to imagine a team member two levels below him at a BBQ on a Sunday. "When they receive an email from the CEO, what do you think that does to their level of relaxation?"

I went on to say that I work for a fantastic firm with an extremely considerate CEO, but if I received an email from him on a weekend, I would absolutely respond. Even if he was insistent that I respond on Monday, I would still spend a good amount of time thinking about the response on my weekend. I asked, "Is this what you are trying to do?"

"No," he replied.

"And yet, this is how people will perceive it. You are saying, by your actions, that this is what you expect of others. There is no "do as I say, not as I do" when you are CEO."

Taking a Public Position

Black Lives Matter, the Ukraine war, conflict in the Middle East, U.S. politics, extreme weather events, and global pandemics—these are important issues that will affect the people in your organization and their families. In their work lives, you are their representative. These people are in your care. So, what is your role as CEO in terms of speaking out on social and political events?

This is one aspect of being CEO that has changed significantly over the last 20 years. There is a pressure and expectation—particularly from employees and society—that didn't exist 20 years ago—that CEOs should publicly comment on these matters.

In a recent survey in the United States of 600 adults, 47% of all respondents said they associated the social, environmental, and political views of CEOs with those of the businesses they lead. A total of 35% said they were more likely to trust brands when they took a stance, with 43% favoring companies that do so on social, environmental, and political issues in particular. In another survey 62% of respondents said that if companies morally disagreed with laws, it's important that they said so publicly.[5]

If you haven't already thought about this, you will need to. It won't take long for something to happen, and you will be expected by some to comment. I am writing this two weeks into the escalation of the Israeli-Palestinian conflict.

I have had conversations with all of my current and many of my former CEO clients about how they deal with what is a charged and complex global social issue. What is their responsibility here? What happens if they take a position now and things happen that make their position change? What is their personal view and is it aligned? Ultimately, as a CEO, should they comment on these things at all?

Whirlpool's Marc Bitzer acknowledges that there are many different views of whether CEOs should take a public position on external events—many of them very strong. It's his view that, as CEO, you need to make a mindful choice about the role you want to be playing publicly. "Every day there is something serious happening, and you have to make a decision," he told me. "You need to be mindful because once you start commenting, people will ask you to comment on everything."

For Marc, this meant making an active decision to only take a public position on Whirlpool itself. "My mindset is that, as CEO, I am here to serve and I am not bigger than my job," he told me. "My responsibility sits within the four walls of the company. The choice I made is that I will not comment on anything that appears on the front page of the *New York Times* because it is lose-lose."

This is one area that keeps CEOs up at night—whether they decide to comment or not, the risk of getting it wrong is significant.

Over the past decade, for example, empathetic leaders have been lauded, and many CEOs have risen to the occasion, particularly during the pandemic. Yet employees are discerning. They want to see true compassion on the issues they and society face, not just lip service. Recent research in the United States found that 52% of employees felt their company's efforts to be empathetic toward employees were dishonest.[6] So, if you are going to take a position, make sure you are doing it because you want to, not because you feel you should. Tread carefully.

Each situation is as different as each organization and CEO. What you decide will depend on many factors. There is no right or wrong answer here. It's another judgment that you will have to make (although there will be no shortage of people telling you what you should do).

One way to think about it is in terms of what issues affect your company, employees, and customers. As UPS CEO Carol Tomé told me, "This is such an important question for all CEOs. My view is that we are not CEOs of companies. We are CEOs of communities, and anybody coming into the role needs to really understand and think through how they will serve in that role."

Carol adopts a simple formula to decide when to speak out as an organization, choosing only to comment when it is part of the company's strategy. "As one of the largest direct-to-consumer businesses, I have one of the most diverse customer bases in the nation, comprising all colors, all ethnicities, all backgrounds, and all beliefs," she told me. "So, we are clear that we should speak on diversity issues because that is representative of our customers."

For example, with the recent Middle East crisis, UPS focused on the humanitarian issues, rather than taking sides, working diligently to get goods into both Israel and Palestine.

Carol noted, "When there was debate in Georgia regarding voting laws, we said, 'We are not red or blue; we are brown' (UPS's corporate color). We didn't take a side, instead we came out with a statement on how we were going to make it easier for our people to vote and how our people would be staffing the polling places. We have tried to turn our points of view into actions that are good for the world and mirror our purpose. This has worked really well for our company."

Carol sees a clear line in terms of the scope of a CEO's obligations in this area. "I have a very good friend who recently retired as CEO who let his personal point of view impact his company's performance because he took stands on things that had nothing to do with the business."

"If you're really convinced about something like that and it is something you want to stand for, then go and stand for it outside of your company," she advised. "Don't drag your company through it. It's not your job."

The New CEO Checklist

- **Own your narrative.** Proactively defining and communicating your story will help the organization understand your vision, values, and strategy. There will be no shortage of people moving to fill the void if you don't do this first.

- **Move quickly on the who, the why, and the what.** In your first days and weeks, everybody in your organization should understand who you are, why you are here, and what you want to achieve. The goal should be to galvanize (and reassure) your organization around your new vision.

- **Prep like a politician**. Have a pre-planned response for questions to avoid the risk of saying something

(continued)

that later comes back to haunt you, and script the first thing and last thing you say in any early presentation.

- **Don't be afraid to say, "I don't know."** You will be under pressure to have a point of view—and to share it. But admitting you don't have all the answers is critical to building trust, promoting collaboration, and encouraging a culture of continuous learning.

- **Remember communication can matter more than actions early on.** There are many examples of CEOs who overlooked this—don't become one of them. Take time to clearly communicate what you are hoping to achieve. Don't think your actions will speak for themselves.

- **Embrace the communication experts.** Your marketing or corporate affairs team can help you craft messages that land well—engage these experts early and hear their advice, particularly if you plan to take a public stand on emerging issues.

CHAPTER 6

Navigating the Crash

"You're riding high in April. Shot down in May . . ."
—Frank Sinatra, "That's Life"

Alan Beacham was six months into the president role at Toll Group, a global logistics and transportation company, when the challenges really began to take hold. "The honeymoon period was over," he told me. "Almost as quickly as we got the first milestone done, I realized that I had an even bigger mountain to climb."

Alan had moved quickly during his transition, identifying the areas of the business that were underperforming, reviewing the organizational structure, and reforming his SLT. But the mountain ahead included steering the company forward on the heels of a global pandemic, which had upended supply chains across the world.

"The outlook when I started was that it would be a difficult six months, then it would all be better," he said. "The reality was it would be a difficult six months and then it would get worse, and then it would almost certainly get worse again the year after. It was like a gradual incline that kept getting steeper and steeper."

Alan was by no means a rookie in the transportation world. But the realities of the new job—and the new business context that Toll Group found itself in—meant he began to question himself. "Are we doing the right things? Is my strategy right? Is my approach right? Is my team right? Are all of these things right?"

For every leader, there comes a point when you crash, when you wonder if you are really up to the challenge—or if you have bitten off more than you can chew. If you are like many other CEOs, you will have this moment more than once across your first 12 months.

You will have days and weeks where you think, "I'm killing it; I'm born to be CEO." Then, very quickly, you take a couple of knocks, and you're thinking, "I cannot do this."

This is a common pattern, and not a bad thing. CEOs who experience this are often more self-aware, humble, and honest with themselves. This is a role like no other, and if you haven't done it before, it is absolutely normal to feel, at least a little, like it is bigger than you.

When I work with clients, this rollercoaster is a frequent subject of conversation. It surprises them regularly through the transition. They say, "I thought I would be better, calmer, or more confident than I am."

Your crash can manifest in any number of areas—the people requirements, the financial responsibility, the impact on your home life, and the breadth and velocity of the decisions you need to make. It can also be due to the complexity and ambiguity in which you need to operate, or the sheer responsibility you now have for the future of this organization and the livelihoods of all the people who work in it.

If you are not experiencing any of this, you might be operating at the surface level and not getting to the crux of the issues. Or your level of self-confidence might be blinding you significantly—the old "fake it till you make it." This could be a considerable blind spot that you might want to explore.

The reality is that no CEO goes through their transition unscathed. When the challenges arrive be attentive, but also kind to yourself, safe in the knowledge that others have struggled and succeeded with the same problems that you now face.

Don't avoid seeking support. I see CEOs who resist help in their transition because they believe it reflects negatively on their readiness or capability. But CEO hubris is a dangerous thing. It can destroy value pretty instantaneously.

The signs of this going badly are generally clear. One CEO whom I almost worked with (this example will explain why it was "almost") resisted help even though the chair, CHRO, and outgoing CEO and founder encouraged him to get transition support.

Six months in, he began making comments like, "I'm the CEO, you have to do what I say," or, "Do I have to remind you that I am the CEO?" This is a classic challenge of confidence. The bravado was masking what was either a complete lack of emotional intelligence or a severe dose of imposter syndrome. A lion doesn't need to tell the other animals it is a lion. Similarly, great leaders don't need to run around announcing their titles either.

If it is your first time as CEO, you were selected because the board was confident that you can do the job, not because you have done it successfully before. Anyone who has experienced the CEO role knows how hard it is—if they are offering help, take it. Be confident that you can grow into being a great CEO, not overconfident that you already have it nailed.

For Alan, this meant being honest with his chair and several board directors. "In a candid discussion, I said, 'Here's the outlook. I can see these challenges and here are the things that are going on. Here's how I think we should respond and I want you to really test me and drill me on this.'"

The advice he got back was that his intuition was, in fact, good. "They told me, 'Don't overthink it. Don't try and over-analyze it. Trust what you know. Do what you need to do and believe in yourself.' Once I accepted that, it became quite liberating. I realized I had nothing to fear."

Power of Reflection

A crash can be an indicator that it's time to pause, take stock, and recalibrate. If you realize this—and take the opportunity—you'll be in a stronger position to find your way to the other side.

If you are like most CEOs in transition, you will be drinking from the fire hose early on, trying to meet as many people as possible, visiting offices or branches, and consuming as much information as you can. You may go at this pace for several months without stopping to reflect on what you are seeing, feeling, learning, and understanding.

The goal is to stop and reflect at least weekly. The work I do with CEOs in transition is a combination of advisory, consulting, and coaching. There are many benefits of having an outside perspective during this time (in my humble opinion, of course), but at the top is how it affords the opportunity for reflection. In particular, these one-on-one meetings force the CEOs to really digest their early experiences— offering a chance to process information, connect patterns, and decipher feedback. If you don't have a coach or advisor, you will need to create the space and time to do this yourself. Schedule time in your calendar accordingly. Journaling can also help during this time.

I can't stress this enough. Don't get to month three or four and realize that you have amassed an enormous amount of information, but have limited understanding. Or that you have analyzed reams of data without unearthing the insights.

When my eldest son learned how to drive, for example, we were very lucky not to have any accidents, although we did have a couple of close calls. When these happened, I didn't brush over them and keep going. Why? Because there would be no learning or development if I did that.

Instead, we discussed the incidents in detail at the end of each drive. In two instances, we stopped driving and did the review there and then to allow for real-time feedback. These moments of reflection are when the lasting learning happens. The time allows for ah-ha moments.

When the inevitable crash bites, it also offers a chance to reset the assumptions and expectations you had of the role—and yourself. Take this opportunity to reflect.

One important step is to make sure you are clear about your priorities and what success looks like from the board's perspective. This is not as easy as it sounds. Asking the board for its expectations of you during the first three to six months is relatively straightforward; drilling into the detail, less so.

I worked with a first-time CEO and asked her chair what success looked like at the three-month mark. Part of his response was that she needed to have formed good relationships with her team.

My role is not to accept this type of high-level answer so I dug deeper, "How would you define a *good relationship*?"

After a challenging 10-minute discussion, the chair was finally able to articulate how he would judge the quality of the relationships, and I was able to convey this to the CEO.

By her own admission, she would not have asked that clarifying question, instead making the assumption that "good" for the chair was the same as it was for her.

Another CEO joined an organization with a 40% attrition rate. The chair had clear expectations the new CEO would significantly reduce the attrition rate. The CEO took this to mean that he had to work with the people he inherited—something he felt would not allow him to drive the changes he thought were needed.

I spoke with the chair and suggested that it was quite normal with a new CEO for there to be some turnover, especially in the SLT. He said, "Of course, I expect him to make the team his own and change those he needs to change, but once that is done, I am expecting a great reduction on the overall attrition rate." Big difference.

So, taking the time to really probe the expectations of your board is fundamentally important. Seek as much clarity as possible—it's what will set you up for success as the new CEO and for your longer-term performance.

Another approach is to realize that you are not infallible as CEO—nor should anybody expect you to be. Among the many challenges of becoming CEO is that there will be things you get wrong. Don't beat yourself up too much. As PepsiCo's CEO Ramon Laguarta explained it, "Making mistakes is part of the job, and there will always be things you wished you'd done differently. But the good news is that you can course-correct."

He continued, "You can optimize over time. It's an optimization of variables that nobody has taught you before, and you have to do it with your own personality, with your own characteristics, so what that looks like is different for everyone. But it can be done."

Here to Serve

A good way to center yourself during a crash, when the chips are down, is to remember why you are here in the first place. By shifting your perspective from yourself to the impact you can have on your organization, you will reignite your passion, confidence, and in turn, your success in the role.

A CEO who was promoted in difficult circumstances found himself a reluctant leader. Part of my role was to help him move past this, so in one of our sessions, we broached his reluctancy by talking about his responsibilities as CEO. When I raised the people in the business, he pre-empted my comment and said, "I know, I know. I am responsible for 120,000 people."

"No," I said, "You are responsible for 120,000 families."

His shoulders slumped and there was a good period of silence while he adjusted his thinking.

The CEO wasn't being flippant. He genuinely cared about the people he was responsible for. He was just struggling to accept the magnitude of the role.

This comment changed the tone of the rest of the conversation, and fortunately for the organization and its 120,000 families, it allowed him to get energized and excited again about being CEO.

In the past, the revered CEO archetype focused on a command-and-control mentality. It was a time when the CEO's word reigned supreme and the title alone garnered respect and deference. Today, great CEOs serve the organizations and the people they lead. They are not there to be served.

Understand and embrace servant leadership—a leadership approach that focuses on the well-being and growth of those around you, whether that's your employees (and their families), your communities, or your customers. In the role of CEO, you are responsible for so much and so many. The best CEOs accept this, adopting a servant mindset and a stewardship approach.

There are many definitions of *servant leadership*, but the most common principles relate to the characteristics of listening, empathy, self-awareness, stewardship, community-building, authenticity, and vulnerability. These skills are increasingly shown to be critical in allowing CEOs to navigate the growing complexity of the job—from pushing ahead with strategic issues like sustainability; tech transformation; or diversity, equity, and inclusion to finding a path forward amid increasing social unrest, geopolitical tensions, and pandemics. But they can also be instrumental in pulling yourself out of the slump—from shifting your perspective from "me" to "we" and helping you remember the purpose you can find in your role.

Finding the Sweet Spot of Vulnerable Leadership By Stephen Langton, Managing Director at RRA

There are people we encounter throughout our careers, personally or via the media, whose leadership styles leave a serious impact on the way we want to lead—whether that's positive ("Now, that's the type of leader I want to be") or negative ("I'm never leading like that").

Over most of the last half-century, the champion CEOs were commonly valorized for their wealth, status, and achievement—their accumulation and status. Things are changing. While success against that profit motive is still celebrated, the reigning CEO ideal has now significantly broadened.

The world demands more from leaders, and today's CEO champions are the ones growing their businesses while also making the biggest social impact, championing diversity, and demonstrating altruism in service of the company and its people.

The old way meant the conditions of success in the organization were almost wholly dependent on the CEO. For today's leaders, it's about installing the conditions for your people to succeed—not being the harbinger of success.

Today, the CEO role model is a vulnerable, realistic human being. Leaders are now stewards of collective success rather than owners of a single vision. But organization-wide empowerment is itself a skill that requires balance.

We know sole ownership, command-and-control leadership isn't wholly suited for today's circumstances. But reckless empowerment without a single guiding force is equally ineffective.

(continued)

The challenge for leaders today now lies in finding the sweet spot: a happy medium in which CEOs install, guide, and maintain systems that empower their employees at every level, while acting as a central driver for the organization's efforts, exerting control where it's useful.

This thinking isn't new or revolutionary. Indeed, like most modern lessons, we just need to look a little further into the past for insight or solutions. Lao Tzu, the Chinese philosopher known for his maxims on successful leadership, said: "A leader is best when people barely know they exist, when their work is done, their aim fulfilled, those they lead will say: we did it ourselves."

Ask yourself, "What type of leader does the organization need me to be at this time?"

Is it the same leader you were in your last role and/or organization?

Great leaders adapt their style to the needs of their respective teams and organizations. At a very junior leader level, it is often the employees who need to fit in with the leader's style. At your level, it is not the case.

As CEO, you will have very bright and capable people in your team, and your responsibility is to create the environment where these people flourish—and in turn, share the load with you.

You will likely have deep experience leading within a function (e.g., finance, marketing, or risk), where there are certain personality types. You now have the whole organization to lead and a much greater variety of personality types. You need to adjust first.

Glass Balls

When RRA asked CEOs how they spent their time with key stakeholders, we found that they invested the least amount of time at home. Topping the list of underappreciated stakeholders were "myself" and "my family/loved ones." A total of 73% and 60% of CEOs said they underinvested their time in these areas, respectively.[1]

In 1991, Bryan Dyson, the then CEO of Coca-Cola, gave a great speech about the importance of balance in life. Using the common expression of "juggling many balls" as a way to express how busy one is, he said that the key to juggling multiple balls was to know which of the balls are made of glass and which are made of rubber.[2]

He explained that health, family, and spirituality were glass balls. The first time you drop them, they don't necessarily break, but they are damaged. If you continue to drop them, they break.

Work is a rubber ball. If you drop it, it bounces right back up. Think of the last "important meeting" that you missed. What happened? Did the company stumble? Did the share price plummet? Were millions lost? I know you are important, but you are not that important. The meeting you missed was probably rescheduled and back in your calendar the next day or next week like nothing had ever happened.

What about the last family event you missed, or sports game, or birthday dinner? Did they replay the game? Did they redo the birthday?

I am being facetious on purpose. Yes, you have a very important role, but please don't lose sight of the truly

(continued)

important things in life. There is time for both—and people want to follow leaders who can get the important events done, both professionally and personally.

One first-time CEO made the decision at the beginning of his transition to send his wife and two young daughters overseas to be with extended family for the first six months of his role, because he had so much to do and would be so busy. He was able to achieve great things but at what cost? That time and that age—you never get back.

Great CEOs are committed to their health and exercise. Regular exercise generates energy and allows you to manage the workload you will face. Many new CEOs get lost in the demands of the role and let this slide only to realize many months down the track that it is a fundamental error. Your role is so demanding that it needs you in prime condition. Your health is key to your ability to do your job well. If you're not sharp and alert, you're useless. Make health a priority. Get plenty of sleep, exercise, and make time for yourself—and your loved ones.

Play Your Position

In Game 6 of the 1980 NBA Championship series between the Los Angeles Lakers and the Philadelphia 76ers, former Lakers' superstar Magic Johnson did something that was both unheard of and spectacular—he played all five positions on the floor during the course of the game and helped LA to clinch the championship (LA was leading 3-2 going into Game 6).

Magic Johnson was a rare player in basketball due to his size, skills, and athleticism. One of only a handful who would be able to comfortably rotate into any of the five playing positions. His decision to do so in Game 6 was not one borne out of ego. It was largely influenced by the absence of an injured Kareem Abdul-Jabbar, LA's superstar center.

While Magic's ability to play all positions helped LA to overcome injury and win the championship, it was not the game plan. It was an emergency decision. Magic was most effective playing as the point guard; that is where he was both most effective for the team dynamic and also the greatest threat to the opposition. Magic knew that, as did the coaching staff.

The same is true for you as CEO.

It is not up to you to play every position on the court. As soon as you can, start focusing on the things only you can (and should) do. This is often easier said than done. The constant challenge many CEOs struggle with every day is resisting getting dragged into tasks, work, and projects that do not fall under the umbrella of the unique contribution of the CEO.

The reason for this is twofold. First, to have been selected as CEO, you likely have a good mixture of deep functional expertise and strong leadership capabilities. As a result you are capable of doing many things really well and even more things averagely well.

Second, as CEO, you also have the ability to get involved with any part of the business—any project at any level—and people will be reluctant to tell you to stay out of things. However, just because you can, doesn't mean you should.

I worked with a CEO who jumped onto projects simply because she enjoyed it. It took six months for the other members to feel comfortable enough to tell her that she was not adding value and her scheduling restrictions for meetings was actually inhibiting the project.

Some of these projects will be because you are asked to get involved. Others will be because you are interested. The former is nice; however it is important to explore why you are being asked to get involved. Is it because your involvement provides safety from accountability for the team? Is it because they lack the understanding/capability/authority to make the decisions? If so, then this is a problem for you to fix.

When we asked more than 200 CEOs globally about the things that only the CEO can or should do, they listed culture (which we cover in Chapter 10), communication (which we cover in Chapter 5), and working with the board (which we cover in Chapter 9). They also cited vision and strategy.[3]

On vision and strategy, I will say this: The long-term future of the organization—what it looks like in 10 years' time—is firmly in your hands.

Something that I remind clients regularly is that as CEO, you are responsible for helping the organization to "lift its head up" and see where it is going. Every time you are talking to the organization, in groups or individually, you have the unique ability to talk about the future, about the vision, about why it is important. For a moment, that individual can look up from the day-to-day work and see down the road.

Interestingly, our research shows that while 54% of CEOs felt they spent the right amount of time on developing the long-term strategy of their organization, 43% said they weren't doing this enough. Similarly, 55% felt they were spending too little time on building innovation capacity, and 67% felt they weren't spending enough time working with other leaders in their industry to solve problems.[4]

Of course, the perennial challenge for many CEOs is balancing a long-term view with more immediate short-term goals. But it's up to you to find the right equilibrium for your organization and navigate the trade-offs around investment decisions. We know that the CEOs who make the most progress on strategic issues like sustainability are those who are able to do this. These leaders possess a great deal of courage—not only to stay the course in the face of setbacks, but to also make decisions that may be unpopular with more short-term orientated stakeholders.[5] Finding this balance is another complex judgment that only you can make, as CEO.

Trust Your Gut

For some CEOs, the crash is not so much a psychological wobble, but an early challenge where you feel the heat from external stakeholders and must find a way forward. But the advice remains the same: take time to reflect, focus on what matters, and do the job that only you can do. Ultimately, only you can pull yourself out of the challenge you're facing. And doing so requires both conviction—and courage.

This happened relatively quickly for Thomas Buberl, who became CEO of global insurance giant AXA in 2016, having previously headed up the company's global health business and German division. Emerging as the frontrunner in the succession process had been a defining moment, yet going on to become CEO turned out to be a humbling experience. "When you go through [a] succession process and obviously you rise to the end of the decision, it feels great," he said on RRA's *Redefiners* podcast. "But then, when you have your first day of office, the counter goes back to zero and you start at the bottom again."[6]

Soon, Thomas was facing 2,000 colleagues, who were looking to him for an inspirational statement of where the company would be going next, as well as investors, regulators, and journalists. It was new territory and caused Thomas to move fast to recalibrate. "I thought, okay, how could I organize myself? [So] I took the two most senior people in the company and said, 'Look, you are my life insurance; you are my deputies, and you need to help me.'"

Thomas also turned to his board and the former CEO. "I had a very good relationship to my board members because they had all chosen me," he said. "And certainly my predecessor, we had a very, very good transition. My predecessor is my best mentor, even to this day."

Thomas was in the fortunate position of taking over the reins of an already successful company. It had, he said, a "great culture and great history." But when he looked at AXA's business profile, he saw that 80% was in life insurance. "At a time where interest rates are low, this is not a great position to be in," he told us. "[So I said] 'Look, what can we do?'"

Thomas moved to shift the company from 80% life insurance to 10% life insurance, all while keeping its €100 billion ($108 billion) revenue steady. It involved some massive transactions—one was quoting a company and buying another company.

"Unfortunately I had to buy before I [could] quote it, which was a very big surprise to the shareholders that said, "What are you doing there? Why do you rock the whole company?" He added, "So we had a massive storm against us by our shareholders, by analysts."

As AXA's share price began to slide, Thomas received a phone call from his predecessors. "They both phoned me and said, "Look, the share price has dropped by 10%. That is a pity. But when I did my big deal, it dropped by 16%. So you are better than I am."

Thomas remained focused and learned to trust his gut. "If you have convictions, and if they are strong, and if your team is behind them, you can master very stormy times," he said.

And that's exactly what happened. In the end, Thomas made AXA even better—not just as a business, but as a positive force in society, even going so far as to remove the company from certain profitable but pernicious industries.

"What's quite interesting is that the same people that criticized this massive transformation are now praising it," he said. "So . . . you need to have a conviction that what [you're doing] is right in the long term, even though it's maybe perceived as being a surprise in the short term."

Reflecting further on the importance of trusting your values in times of challenge, Thomas continued, "In a very uncertain time, when things are foggy, [and] you don't know what to do next . . . my mantra is just follow your gut. It means following your values, following your principles . . . Be yourself. You will find the right answer."

The New CEO Checklist

- **Know this is normal.** Every CEO faces a moment when they crash—whether through a lack of confidence or clarity, exhaustion, or a challenging business

(continued)

context. Remember that, just like the others who have gone before you, you can (and will) overcome it.

- **Take the opportunity to recalibrate.** It's likely you are crashing because you have not taken time to reflect, invest in yourself, or seek enough clarity from your board. Take this moment for what it is: a chance to course-correct—and come out stronger.

- **Look in *and* out.** Self-reflection is critical in moments of crisis. But there comes a time when you need to look beyond your struggles and focus on why you are here in the first place. You are here to serve. Focusing on this can help reignite your purpose and your passion.

- **Don't neglect your health, family, or friends.** This role is not to be done at the expense of these important things. As important as you now are, you are completely replaceable at work. However, you are not replaceable to your loved ones. And they are often the ones who can help pull you out of the crash.

- **Narrow your aperture.** Too many CEOs exhaust themselves because they are focused on trying to do it all, instead of relying on the strengths of their team. Don't be one of them. Focus on the things that only you can do—typically culture, communication, interacting with the board, and vision and strategy.

- **Find the solution within.** As Thomas Burberl made clear, trust your gut. By surrounding yourself with the right people and trusting your convictions, you will find the right answers.

PART III

Up and Running:
Early Priorities

CHAPTER 7

Building Your Top Team

"The best leaders are those most interested in surrounding themselves with what is best and brightest."

—Lao Tzu, philosopher

When Doug Mack started as CEO at Fanatics in 2014, he hadn't realized that fixing the company's culture would be one of his immediate priorities—and biggest challenges. Over the past two decades, Fanatics had transformed from a mall retail store in Jacksonville, Florida, to a major e-commerce retailer of official sports merchandise, with $800 million in revenues.

Doug's appointment was a natural fit. Not only was he a life-long sports fan, he'd also spent his career powering businesses forward—having founded a rich-media platform (later sold to Adobe), before going on to helm One Kings Lane, the luxury-home décor business.

He was ready for the role and was looking forward to doubling down on the customer experience to fuel the company's next phase of epic growth. But the culture at Fanatics came as a big surprise. "When you think about a digital upstart like Fanatics, your competitive advantage should be your team spirit, your camaraderie, and your hunger for speed, but we didn't have any of it," Doug told me. "There was no bond that tied everyone together. In fact, our people talked about one another like they were from different companies."

In some ways they were: over the past two years, Fanatics had made a series of acquisitions that had allowed it to scale significantly, but had also left it struggling to unite its 2,000 employees that were now sprawled across the United States.

"It was just shockingly Balkanized," Doug told me. "There was a lack of trust and a lack of partnership. That's really rare for a company that's still in that emerging scaling space."

He said, "I remember sitting in a hotel room in Jacksonville after my first week thinking: 'This is going to be a real challenge.' Not in a bad way, but there was just so much that needed to be addressed. For me, your culture can never be good enough."

This was Doug's third time in the CEO seat, and he was clear from the start that the culture was going to be a major roadblock to growth—and that he needed to move quickly to fix it. He set his sights on the top of the house, making sure he had the right team around him that would serve as a beacon for the culture that he wanted to instill.

In his first 90 days, with advice he'd received years earlier from Marrissa Mayer, the former CEO of Yahoo!, still ringing in his ears, he made three changes to his executive team.

"She had told me that you shouldn't wait too long to make the changes you think are needed—and that advice stayed with me," Doug said. "I'm Midwestern, I'm people-oriented, I have a high EQ. But I've also kind of learned that if you have somebody who's holding the team back you have to make the change as soon as you know."

In the end, Doug changed around 80% of the top team in his first 18 months. "To me, being a CEO is all about being the coach of a team of elite players." He continued, "The foundation was to get the full new team built, blending strong incumbent executives with new hires, so we were ramping up together. Because if you build your top team well, they give you leverage because they begin building their teams well, and you get a cascading effect."

When I met with Doug, he was getting ready to step down as CEO of Fanatics and begin his retirement, having grown the company tenfold over 10 years, posting revenues approaching $8 billion.[1] Today, Fanatics is a sports e-commerce powerhouse, with 900 global sports partners, ranging from the NFL to the NBA to Notre Dame to Chelsea and the Tokyo Giants.

"I'm now having investment bankers tell me that different companies are claiming they're going to be the Fanatics of their industry, which is the ultimate compliment," Doug smiled.

* * *

For years, it was thought that being a great CEO was enough to power organizational performance. It's what led to the rise of "hero CEOs" in corporate folklore—leaders valorized by employees, investors, and the media for their talent for changing companies' fortunes. Of course, as CEO, you are still the core player in delivering organizational success (that will never change), but it's no longer the whole story.

The issues facing organizations are now more complex than ever before. As CEO, you're under pressure to navigate new threats that are emerging at breakneck speed, all while future-proofing your business model and securing competitive advantage.

You need the right people and team around you—as Doug was clear about from the start.

Your SLT is one of the greatest levers you have as CEO. It is through your SLT that you will be able to, or not be able to, deliver on the promises you make to the board, shareholders, market, and importantly, the organization.

As such, your success (and legacy) as a CEO depends on your ability to build and lead a high-performing C-suite at the individual and team levels. Doing so will require vision, courage, and more than a few difficult choices.

But as one CEO, a first-time external hire, put it to me, "You can only go as fast as the slowest member of your team, so until you get that right, your ability to move at pace will be restricted."

So, do it you must. How you go about that is what we'll be covering in this chapter and the next.

Move Fast on Your Team

At several points in this book you read about the benefits of slowing down, of taking time to learn the context before making major decisions.

However, the area where speed is encouraged is in decisions about your team. Here, moving fast is widely touted as the better choice.

The reflection I hear most from the CEOs I work with is that you cannot move quickly enough on your team. In my recent research on CEO transitions, 65% said their top transition regret was that they did not move faster on building their top team (86% of experienced CEOs listed it as their top regret, 75% of externally recruited first-time CEOs, and 38% of internally promoted first-time CEOs).[2]

In terms of timing, 48% made the first change to their team within the first three months. A further 26% made it in the second three months.[3]

Often, CEOs get a good read early on their team, and instead of acting, they wait to give the people and the organization more time. This, in hindsight, causes more issues, and delays the CEO from being able to deliver and perform.

The CEOs who were generally happy with how quickly they moved adopted the following plan: in their first month, they assessed the team. In the second, they decided how the team should be structured and who should be on it. And in the third, they made the changes. (Although many also admitted they could have moved even faster.)

Why do people wait? There are generally a number of answers. Here are the top six reasons that I see. Going into your transition with these in mind may help you avoid this common trap and the most-cited regret of your CEO peers.

- **Grace.** As the new CEO, you accept that there is much you don't know, especially around people. So, you give them grace, often against your gut instinct, and more than you should.

- **Guilt.** You recognize that this is an existing team of people, each with families and responsibilities. You feel bad that your appointment as CEO means that some may lose their jobs.

- **Best behavior.** The arrival of a new CEO gives poor performers a chance for a reprieve—and as a result, they are on their best behavior. You see a motivated, engaged executive, but the organization generally knows better. You are their last chance.

- **Savior complex.** You think, "I'm a good leader, good enough to make this poor performer better, I can save them." This is often more about your ego than reality. Your responsibility is the organization. You can inspire and motivate people, but you are not responsible for saving them. (The risk of above-average bias.)

- **Gun shy.** This is common. We have all experienced or heard about the new "hatchet" CEO who comes in and lobs heads immediately. It is not an enviable perception, so some CEOs who really should wield the hatchet, don't. In delaying, they slow the success of the entire organization, and importantly, their success as CEO.

- **"Okay" performance.** The leader might not be a poor performer. But they are not the right fit for you, the team you want to build, or the way you want to lead. Many CEOs hope that this "good person" becomes the "right person." In my experience, they rarely do. And what should have been a positive exit with an obvious trigger (a new CEO) ends up becoming a painful performance issue.

Decide How You Will Assess Your Team

So, you need to move fast. But how do you make the judgment call about the leaders you want to stay and potentially develop, and the leaders you need to replace. How will you assess your team? What measures will you use?

As CEO, you will have no shortage of data for every decision or problem you face. Ideally, this will also be the case with your SLT in terms of assessment and performance data. Commonly, CEOs will make effective use of this data alongside trusting their instincts.

You have years of experience in making judgments on people, in all aspects of your life as well as in business. You have an array of good, bad, and ugly experiences over your career, and this will have refined your internal (gut) assessment. If your initial feeling is that this person is not the right one, either due to attitude, motivation, capability, or simply fit for your leadership style, and this feeling does not pass in the first several interactions, then act on it. The other thing that comes up for CEOs is the question of trust: "Person X is really good, capable, and well liked, but I just do not trust them." Replace them. You cannot have people on your team whom you do not trust. You simply will not succeed as CEO. As you look at your new team, ask yourself, "Do I trust this leader?" If "yes," then great. If "no," you know what you need to do—and do quickly.

Your SLT is so important that you can't have "maybes", or if you do, you can't have them for very long. You can't have people in the boat that you are unsure are rowing, or worse still, are dragging their oar. Or as one CEO described it,

"Three of my SLT were sitting in the boat drilling holes in the bottom."

When CEOs describe members of their team as "good" or "okay," I will sometimes push and ask them, "Is good really good enough? What are you sacrificing for the organization's success of having a key role filled by a role player instead of a star?" Of course, I am well aware of the importance of role players and that a team of stars can be (and often is) bettered by a star team—just make sure that is what you have, and that your "good" isn't the enemy of great.

Leadership Span™

At RRA, we help CEOs go beyond the gut feel for decisions, employing psychometric data to help understand an existing leaders' strengths and weaknesses, or incoming leaders' readiness for the C-suite.

The model we use is Leadership Span™, which assesses whether executives are able to flex their approach.

As my colleague Erin Zolna, who leads our Assessment offering at RRA, explained, "The best executives are able to bring different skills to the fore, depending on the specific situation they face. They embody both 'loud' and 'quiet' competencies. They show both rational and emotional intelligence. And they are able to handle contradictory, sometimes conflicting, ideas simultaneously."

Through empirically validated research, we found the most effective leaders typically span four dualities.

- **Being both disruptive and pragmatic.** Great leaders know when to disrupt the status quo with innovation, and when to be pragmatic about focus, priorities, and the pace of transformation.

- **Being both risk-taking and reluctant.** Great leaders know when to take calculated risks and be opportunistic, and when to show vigilance before steering the organization off a cliff.
- **Being both heroic and vulnerable.** Great leaders are heroic, but they are also vulnerable, knowing how to ensure perseverance and grit don't turn into self-delusions. They take feedback and external data to heart and make continuous improvements to themselves and their organizations.
- **Being both galvanizing and connecting.** Great leaders galvanize support with energy and inspiration, but they also know when to take a step back, share credit, and promote the success of others. They can connect the organization to become something stronger and greater than themselves and the cult of their own personality.

The ideal situation is to utilize a psychometric assessment tool (as most of the featured CEOs in this book did) to ensure that you are countering your biases (and those of the organization) and to help you have a base assessment that allows you to compare apples with apples, as the saying goes.

Hans Vestberg, CEO of Verizon and former CEO of Ericsson, adopts this approach to assessing his teams when he starts as CEO, working with a third party to stop any biases that he (or the existing leadership or HR function) may bring to the table. "Talent decisions are so crucial that I put everyone through a formal assessment process—it was and still is essential that I was able to understand if we have the right people in the right roles," he told me. "The intent is to make sure that their capability and skill are being assessed today and for the business that I want to build."

He added, "When I did this at both Verizon and Ericsson, it did lead to people leaving the organization, but we also found that, in many cases, we had the right person in the wrong role."

From my research, the following areas were identified as common when CEOs reflect on what they look for when assessing their SLT during their transition.[4] At the team level, they look at the team dynamics—how the members work together, how decisions are made, the level of trust as it relates to debate and the outputs. At the individual level, the traits CEOs most commonly look for are: motivation/energy/purpose, capability/capacity, openness/transparency, collaboration, curiosity/intellect, commerciality, and scalability.

Of course, you need to create plenty of opportunities for you to develop a gut feel for your leaders' performance. One tactic is via off-sites (as we'll see UPS CEO Carol Tomé did at her home in North Georgia in Chapter 8). Another is to increase the cadence of the SLT meetings. This gives you more opportunities early on to see the team behave, interact, perform, and communicate. Essentially more time on the ground here helps you to ensure you have seen what you need, good or otherwise.

The approach I see many CEOs adopt when relying on their gut feeling is to apply the simple concept of "skill versus will" or "attitude versus aptitude." The idea is that if a leader has the right will or attitude, but lacks certain skills, then it's a positive, providing the skill gap can be closed quickly. If it cannot, you might have the right person in the wrong job. It's a common issue and fixable.

If a leader has the skills, but not the will, then it's usually a very short conversation that goes something like: "Is this the right role and organization for you?"

As a check process, ask questions like:

- Do they know what is expected of them?
- Do they have the tools and resources, plus the opportunity, to build skills and use them effectively?
- Are they surrounded by aligned people?

It is really challenging to decide that people who have worked at an organization for a period of time should no longer work there—just because you think it to be the case. It is tough, but necessary.

It is normal to be reluctant around these changes.

The Power of Wide *T*-Shaped Leaders
By Laura Sanderson,
Managing Director at RRA

The challenges and opportunities that are coming to define the first half of the 21st century like sustainability, Gen-AI, and tech transformation do not touch just one function or business line at a time. As CEO, solving those problems will require you to identify and assess for C-suite leaders who can work horizontally across the company as well as vertically in their function or business line. We call them wide *T*-shaped leaders.

These are leaders who can combine "enterprise thinking" with deep business line or functional expertise. The typeface of the *T* is also important. A narrow *T* is one where the horizontal enterprise thinking line is narrow and the vertical

(continued)

functional line is long. This represents a leader who is deep in their function, but narrow in their enterprise thinking across the wider business.

A wide *T* leader is the opposite. Think of the kind of *T* that would not look out of place on an American college sweatshirt. These leaders are wide in their enterprise thinking and understanding of the other functions around them. They may be less deep in their own functional or business line expertise. This is a good position for a C-suite executive, especially if they aspire to succeed you one day as CEO.

When people describe an executive as being capable of "enterprise thinking," what they are often saying is that they have the instinct and ability to consider how decisions impact the wider business and connect to the strategy. This mindset allows them to make balanced assessments, take actions that do not inhibit the organization's ability to succeed, and mitigate any unintended consequences of decisions.

You can no doubt think of many examples of decisions that benefit one function or area while inhibiting another. There was a story of an airline that decided to incentivize pilots based on fuel usage and ground crews on turnaround times for the planes. However, they did so without an enterprise mindset. The pilots altered flight paths to catch strong tail winds, often coming in late, but with fuel savings. The ground crews struggled to turn the planes around to achieve the departure times. Both were great incentives in isolation, but counterintuitive collectively.

So, as you look to build your top team, work with your leadership advisor of choice to seek out and assess for *T*-shaped leaders. The leaders wearing the wide T-shirt will prove to be the ones who can drive enterprise performance, and consequently who will define your personal success as CEO.

Would You Rehire?

When I am working with CEOs during the early stages of their transition, and we are discussing their team, there is one question that I always ask, "Knowing what you know now about your leaders, if they applied for this role again, would you rehire them?"

There are three possible responses, although I often hear a fourth.

- **An unequivocal and immediate "yes."** This is a team member whom the CEO is supremely confident is the right person in the right role at the right time.

- **An equally quick "no."** This is a clear-cut reaction. But it is often the first time the CEO has verbalized this thought, so it can be confronting.

- **A pause.** This is almost always a "no."

- **A "that's a great question."** This is just a clever way to pause or deflect. The result is often a "no."

Remember, some CEOs give trust upfront and let leaders erode it. Others offer nothing upfront, instead requiring their leaders to earn every bit of trust the hard way. Which are you? What about your team?

Understanding this early (and being transparent about your preferences) can remove some friction points. If you are the latter, the lesson from this is that you need to create opportunity for the members of your team to demonstrate they are trustworthy. Some CEOs will do this via off-sites; others will do it via presentations or attendances at the board meetings. Either way, where possible, you need to create opportunities early in your transition to see what your team is really like.

Make Your Decision, But Be Aware of the Prevailing View

As part of your assessment of SLT members, it is beneficial to take time to understand the prevailing view.

If the board, chair, CHRO, or executive team have a view that an executive is not performing, be mindful of that. Remember that, in some cases, people will behave or perform better when a new leader arrives, almost like a death-row reprieve. This boost in behavior or performance, or both, is generally temporary.

You need to consider whether you want to save someone who the board or organization thinks should be gone. If everyone thinks this person is underperforming, you need to be really sure before you throw them a lifeline. Otherwise, the perception will be that "you clearly do not see things like the rest of us, maybe *you* are not a great fit."

Sometimes opinions from the board, CHRO, or executive teams might not be forthcoming. It is up to you to mitigate this risk.

One CEO I advised had recently taken over a large regional business in a multinational company. A member of her executive team had twice been on a performance management plan. The group CEO and group CHRO, plus the regional CHRO, had decided to not say anything, but instead let the incoming CEO make her own determination about who was good or otherwise.

The official message was one of good intent: we don't want to influence her decision; it is her team, and she should make her own mind up on the people and structure. Yet I also believe there was an underlying malintent of, "Let's see if she see things like we do; let's see if she spots him"—a test.

As the new CEO started to learn the business, the region, and the people, she did not get an opportunity to really put this individual to the test. At the same time, the poor performer was, like the rest of the executive team, on their best behavior.

When the CEO and I discussed her team early on, she had heard murmurs about this individual, but commented that she had found him really positive and proactive. Then, in the stakeholder feedback, the true feeling and history came out, so I was able to report back to her that this individual was a "dead man walking" as far as the organization was concerned and that they were waiting to see if she saw it, too.

She still felt that he showed promise. We talked about whether this was a hill she was willing to die on because the downside seemed to outweigh the upside. Is it really a win if you prove the organization wrong about a person they are clear is not a good fit for the business? Ultimately, she agreed and removed him, plus two others.

Focus on the Roles, Not the People

One mistake some new CEOs make is to get trapped working roles around the existing people. It is generally best practice to look at the roles and structure without the people who currently occupy the roles.

When you assess leadership in your company, there are generally three parts to consider:

1. What leadership capabilities do we need?
2. What leadership capabilities do we have?
3. How do we plug the gaps?

(continued)

This is best practice. Where some CEOs fall short is starting at number two, instead of number one due to the pressure around the existing people, then realizing months down that track that they do not have the right structure for the organization. Of course, there are always considerations around the continuity of corporate knowledge (knowing where the bodies are buried). You don't want to grind your organization to a halt. However, you also need to keep focused on developing a structure that will serve the organization longer term.

Ask yourself, "What kind of senior team is needed? What knowledge, experiences, skills, attributes, and attitudes are important?" Sometimes you don't need to replace people, but merely realign their roles and responsibilities. A good tip is to draw the ideal organizational structure with no names in the boxes so you can test what the functions and roles are independent of the people who sit in them.

On the Right Tack

Identifying the right members for your team is just the start. Star players are one thing, but what you really need is a star team. For this reason, you need to make sure you are setting up your leaders in the right way so they all pull in the same direction toward your strategic vision. We explore this in detail in the next chapter, and discuss some of the many ways of doing this. But, first, I wanted to share how one CEO, Winnie Park at Forever 21, has tackled this end-to-end—and how storytelling has served as a powerful tool to help her connect and align her SLT around a new future.

Just months before the global pandemic upended the retail sector across the world, Forever 21 filed for bankruptcy.

Once a darling of shopping malls across the world, the retailer had struggled to maintain its grip on sales amid fierce competition from other fast-fashion brands. Two years after it was bought out by SPARC Group for $81 million, Winnie Park took the helm.

Described at the time by Marc Miller, CEO of SPARC Group, as an "inspirational leader and team builder," Winnie wasted little time assembling her top team. As a second-time CEO, she knew that working quickly and decisively on her SLT would be key for the company's turnaround to succeed.

For Winnie, it wasn't so much a building of a team, but a rebuilding. "I wanted to draw on the strengths of the leaders who had steered the company from its inception, through bankruptcy, and out the other side," she told me, 18 months into the role. "They were clear leaders of the business, not only in terms of what they contributed, but also in their historical knowledge and as leaders of hearts."

That's not to say hard decisions weren't made. Winnie assessed the team through the lens of both purpose and culture, and in some cases, this meant swapping out leaders in critical positions. The result was a team that would help turn around the company.

The next challenge was how Winnie could, as the new CEO, "get these talented people to play well together." "I use this analogy at Forever 21, which is we're on a sailboat," she told me. "I know other CEOs like football analogies or basketball, but I find people can more easily imagine sailing." She continued:

> I like this analogy because in sailing everybody works. You've got a destination, but the environment is unknown. It's the same in business. You and your team need to adjust, to tack, to reef the sails, or even batten

down the hatches. But whatever you do, everyone has to do it together. There is something beautiful about being part of a crew, choosing to board a vessel, and be part of the work and the journey.

If you can get everybody on that sailboat working for the same end, dealing with the weather and the conditions together, and understanding that it's not a straight line to the destination, that is a beautiful thing. The best part about being a CEO is when you can see that happening.

The New CEO Checklist

- **Move fast on your team.** Having the right team around you is paramount to your success as CEO. Those who are happy with how quickly they moved spent their first month assessing their team and their second deciding how the team should be structured and who should be on it. By the third month, they had made their changes.

- **Watch out for decision delayers.** Don't avoid making the decisions you need to out of guilt or a savior complex—okay performers are not great performers, and they will hold you back. Watch out for SLT members who see you as their last chance, and are on their best behavior.

- **Collect your evidence.** This will likely be a combination of psychometric assessment data and gut feeling. Remember, you'll need to provide plenty of opportunities to see your team members' true colors—whether through off-sites or additional meetings. And don't forget to understand the board's and your SLT's prevailing views.

- **Look for future-ready leaders.** The world is changing. Your SLT must change with it. To rise to the challenges of sustainability, tech transformation, and other strategic issues, you'll need wide *T*-shaped leaders who combine functional expertise with an enterprise mindset.

CHAPTER 8

Leading Your Top Team

"Lay out the ground rules early. If you don't, you're playing a game where no-one knows the rules."
—Marc Bitzer, CEO of Whirlpool

C arol Tomé hadn't been searching for a new job when she stepped down as CFO at Home Depot after 18 years in the role. But when the CEO position became vacant at the global shipping company UPS, it had felt like a "straightforward choice"—not least because she'd sat on its board since 2003.

"I knew that UPS was an amazing organization with a powerful brand, a culture and values perfectly aligned with my own, operations in more than 220 countries and territories, and roughly half a million talented employees whom I hoped to inspire around a shared purpose," she wrote in the *Harvard Business Review*. "Because the company's stock had been flat for six years, there was also an opportunity to create value for shareholders. And, frankly, my husband was keen to get me out of the house and working again."[1]

Yet the decision turned out to be a little less straightforward than planned, with Carol accepting the role in March 2020, just at the point when Covid-19 reached the shores of Europe, Africa, North America, and South America, and was on the cusp of becoming a global pandemic.

When I met Carol three years later, she had successfully steadied the ship and steered it through to the other side. "It was a crazy time for everybody," she recalled. "It was chaos. People were running down the halls. And I was like, 'What is this?'" She continued, "This is not how you run a business. You don't run it in chaos. You understand the problem. You take it apart and build it back together. Then you put together a plan."

At the same time, Carol was acutely aware of the fear and anxiety that a new CEO can generate across an organization—not least because she was the first outside CEO in UPS's 113-year history. She moved quickly to hold a meeting at her Covid-safe home in north Georgia, where the team could talk openly about how they were going to work together, the behaviors that would be welcomed, and those that would not.

"It was like you're at my house, you're part of my family," she told me. "Everyone got a chance to talk. People wrote down how they felt about the company. Then we had a big bonfire and those letters were burned. It was very cathartic."

For Carol, it was an exercise where she listened more than she talked. She had a point of view on how the company could turn the economic dials to create more value and move the stock price. But she first wanted to hear from the team.

"I have learned that engaging for impact is really important," she told me. "I'm super curious; I ask a lot of questions. I don't criticize. People responded well, saying, 'Wow, she actually wants to understand.'"

As she told *Harvard Business Review*, Carol also had her senior leaders reflect on where the company was spending its time. Sitting in a conference room, she handed out colored stickers and asked everyone to put one next to UPS's top strategic projects—red for stop, green for continue.

"Green dots went up immediately, but people seemed hesitant to dole out red ones. I told them they couldn't leave the room until they did. And lo and behold, once all the stickers had been placed, we realized that we were pursuing some initiatives and activities that didn't promise to add a lot of value. We realized that we should shift money away from the reds and into the greens, and doing so paid off."

Reflecting on the results of her early transition, she said: "We strategized. We reorganized. We prioritized. We divested. We invested. And I believe we've come out of it with a stronger, more engaged team."[2]

* * *

What Carol did so well was to establish new and clear ground rules for how her top team would operate, almost from Day One. She didn't criticize, she didn't point out deficiencies, but she did corral them around a new vision that set the stage for how they would win—together, as a team.

Your organization is made up of multiple teams, but none have the ability to impact the organizations performance, or your performance, like the SLT.

How your top team operates—whether they pull together to support your vision, or pull apart—comes largely down to *your* actions. The expectations that *you* set, the tone that *you* establish.

There are a whole suite of actions that you can take to unleash the true potential of your top team, which we explore in this chapter—from how you show up as a leader, as well as your ability to flex your leadership style, and strike the right balance between making your authority clear while also not unduly influencing debates.

But one of the first steps you can take as soon as you have the majority of your team in place is to invest in team-building. You need to drive this and stay on it. How your SLT operates will be a reflection of you and a key assessment point for the board and external parties on the quality of your leadership.

Off-sites and other team dynamics initiatives are critical, but they are not something you can run yourself—you'll need outside help, so you can also go through the process and learn about what *you* need to do differently, as well as the team.

Establish a "First-Team" Mentality Early

No team is more important than your SLT. It is impossible for you to be successful without the right people around you, thinking and acting in the right way.

One of the first questions I ask my clients when working with them on this is, "Do your executive team members see each other as their first team?"

In many cases, the answer will be "no." Many executives do not see the SLT as their first team. Instead, they believe their first team is the team they are responsible for managing. A CFO, for example, will often see the finance team below as their first team.

This is a problem. When senior leaders are only thinking about representing the team working below them—to fight for that team, to secure resources and allowances, as well as benefits and rewards for them, it can lead to a more adversarial relationship with their peers on the SLT. The exact opposite of what is needed to create a high-performing top team.

Winnie Park, the CEO of Forever 21, uses this concept and the language of "the first team" to drive her SLT performance. "As a cross-functional team with individuals who have grown up in functional silos, they need to see each other as their first team," she said. "You respond to each other's requests first; you talk all the time; you have each other's backs."

I have seen SLT members struggle to decide where they should sit in the building. Do they sit with their functional team or do they sit with the CEO and the rest of the SLT? This might seem trivial, but it is a good example of the internal conflict executives can experience around this. In all cases, the right answer for these leaders was to sit with the CEO and their peers. In most cases, the leader of the functional team they were managing below endorsed their decision and appreciated that it was the right thing for the function and the organization.

Changing your executives' mindsets about their first team is often a significant shift. It may be a challenge for some to accept—especially those who have attached part of their identity to their role as a functional leader, to fiercely defend their team and support their progress and development. Yet embracing this change will have a dramatic impact on the performance of the organization *and* your performance as CEO.

The differences it can make to how senior leaders act, think, and behave is enormous. Relationships become deeper and discussions richer.

Once you've flown the flag for helping your top team see each other as their first team, it's good practice to find ways to continually reinforce it. This practice is even better if you can get to a point where it becomes self-regulating.

I encouraged a CEO I advised to use the concept of "above-the-line" and "below-the-line" thinking and behavior. "The line" represents the SLT level, so "above-the-line" refers to the enterprise thinking and behaviors expected from the first team, while "below-the-line" relates to "functional" thinking and behaviors. Every time discussions started to get off course, the CEO (or one of the SLT members) would ask, "Is this an above-the-line or below-the-line discussion or thought process?" It meant the team quickly became comfortable to be challenged, and in a short period of time, were functioning very differently as a SLT.

I have seen some CEOs actively work against this concept, working to keep tension and competition in their SLT. They want members to fight for resources, to challenge each other's ideas and suggestions, and not think as a unit. While less common, I have also seen CEOs who, in my view, are trying to divide and conquer, in an attempt to protect themselves from challenge.

Productive Tensions

At RRA, we believe that members of high-performing top teams have five common requirements: absolute trust, mission alignment, strategy adaptation, a focus on results, and established team norms. They have respect for each other and know how to work together—but most importantly, they know *why* they are working together. They have a defined team purpose directly aligned with the achievement of the organization's goals and know how to challenge and support each other in reaching them.

And the payoff for getting it right? RRA's research shows that when CEOs believe they are surrounded by a high-performing team, they say they are 42% more effective at managing complex initiatives, and 27% better at delivering on strategic priorities.[3] That's a lot of upside!

We help clients achieve what we call *Productive Tensions* in their executive teams, which captures the four essential trade-offs that top teams need to navigate, including how the CEO leads the group.[4] A key tenet of Productive Tensions is that there is no static definition of a good top team. Instead, top teams face an obligation to constantly recalibrate priorities as organizational and market conditions change.

- **Adaptability:** The top team balances the creation of new growth opportunities or business models while simultaneously focusing on continuous improvement and incremental innovations on existing products and services.
- **Perspective:** The top team drives the organization toward a long-term and sustainable competitive advantage

(continued)

in the market, while continuing to win in the current environment and deliver near-term value.

- **Atmosphere:** Executive leaders capitalize on the dynamics of the top team through trust, collaboration, and conflict resolution, while harnessing ambitions, perspectives, and competitive spirit to drive enterprise-wide outcomes.
- **Team leader:** Specific to the CEO, this category focuses on self-awareness regarding their leadership capabilities and approaches, and the ability to flex to the team's context and needs, while also maintaining decisiveness to influence the team's performance.

Every executive team is made up of a diverse mosaic of personalities, each with their own style, behaviors, and expertise, and each focused on delivering their own set of goals and priorities. Tensions are inevitable. But in the most successful senior leadership teams, everyone pulls in the same direction to deliver against your strategy and vision. Executives have respect for each other and are passionate about working together to drive results.

Of course, this cohesion does not mean that the team is homogenous in its thinking or unwilling to engage in vigorous debate and disagreement. Competition and challenge, discourse and debate, challenge and passion are all important aspects of any team. There are really positive ways to do this (and you need to do this for a team to be truly effective), but if you do this in a way that separates and creates a divide that results in your team not acting like a team, then you have firmly shot yourself in the foot, leg, and likely stomach.

So, take the time to understand how your SLT perceives their first team (not just the niceties that they tell you—do they really believe it and live it?). You need to be certain they put the company's needs above those of their function, business unit, or division. Are they coming to represent their function to the company, or are they here to represent the company to their function or divisions? Address this early and often. Having a leadership team that thinks like this produces significantly different results than one that is trying to "win for their function" over the enterprise. Not all executives can make this shift. Move on the ones who cannot or will not.

Different Strokes for Different Folks

As CEO, you lead the most important team in the entire organization. These are the organization's top executives (behind yourself). They are the best in their area that you have, and they are potentially all very different. This can often be a real test for new CEOs.

If you have become CEO from a specific functional expertise, it is possible that you have only ever led people within that function your entire career. You may be a great leader and have led (and built) high-performing teams, but if those teams consisted of all the same types of people, managing a diverse executive team will offer new and different challenges.

Your executive team will be made up of leaders with different areas of expertise—marketing, finance, legal, HR, tech, and so on. You are now responsible for each of these areas. This can create challenges from two dimensions.

First, the technical aspects: do you understand the function enough to spot good from bad, to be able to make decisions, and importantly, to be able to add the value you should as CEO?

Second, how will you navigate the different thinking styles and cognitive models? People from different functions typically think in different ways. Someone with a finance background may think differently to someone with a marketing one—whether innately or by virtue of their learned career experiences.

It is now well understood that this diversity of thought, coupled with the diversity of members, delivers better decisions and outcomes (one McKinsey study found, that organizations in the top quartile for gender diversity on executive teams were 25% more likely to achieve above-average profitability).[5]

Yet, dealing with this mosaic of personalities and thinkers will require you to be able to adapt your style and approach. You'll need to work hard to help maintain the diverse voices on your SLT and not create your very own echo chamber.

Biases are discussed in Chapter 3, and there is another one you need to be aware of as you transition to CEO: biased thinking around your area of functional expertise. I call this "functional bias."

If during the course of your career, you have held general management or P&L roles, then this may be less of a blind spot for you. However, if you became CEO by moving directly from a functional role, it can lead to you leaning too heavily on this experience.

An example was a CFO I worked with who was promoted to CEO in a company she had worked for many years. Her deep understanding of and reliance on the numbers meant that her default response when challenged was "to check the numbers." The issue was that the board started to lose confidence that she could break her CFO mindset and truly become the enterprise leader they needed her to be.

Another way that functional bias can manifest is by prioritizing the function you used to work in, while downgrading others due to a lack of understanding or confidence.

For example, one CEO I worked with had been promoted from the COO role. For the past six years, he'd competed with marketing for resources and in his words "giving them a hard time." Now he found himself responsible for the function and struggled for more than a year to feel like he appreciated the nuances of the function enough to be supportive and add value.

One way to deal with functional bias is to very consciously lean into the functions you are least comfortable with, and lean back from the one where you have the most technical expertise.

Leading Former Peers

If you have been promoted to CEO, you will likely find yourself leading some of your former peers. You may even find yourself leading some of your former leaders.

Leading former peers is a regular challenge at all levels. It involves the change of a relationship from equal, and in some cases friend, to boss. Plus, there may be disappointment or jealously around your promotion—or even a perception that the decision was unfair or plain wrong.

When the succession process is transparent and clearly explained, leading peers can be relatively positive. People may still leave simply because they wanted to be CEO and

(continued)

having missed out they will now pursue the role elsewhere. If it has been a fair process, they will likely leave well.

However, there may be members of your new team who applied or wanted your role, or who feel that they are better placed to do it (these are different). In most cases, you will find they choose to leave or you decide that you want them to leave. Your promotion has changed the career path for many people in the organization, and so it is normal and natural that some will begin to look elsewhere.

Remember that you need the right team around you, and whether they self-select out or you push them out, it means that they are not right. Sometimes CEOs can get caught out by not wanting to come across as a hatchet bearer, but the reality is that change brings change.

Another dynamic to watch out for is the relationship with former peers whom you opposed or competed with on areas such as resource allocation and strategic choices. Discuss this early in your one-on-ones, raise it, and address how it will change now, and be clear about what your expectations are of that individual and what they should expect from you. Personal differences aside, they may be valuable assets to the firm. Assess them like you would the rest of your leadership team. It will help counter any biases you may have about them.

Showing Up Consistently

As CEO, you are no doubt aware that you cast a long shadow over the organization—and you work hard to show up in the right way in Town Halls and All-Hands. What I often see many CEOs overlook is the importance of extending this same attitude to every SLT interaction. At some point, you will let your guard down, whether through a lapse in judgment, overfamiliarity, or in the case of our former CEO Clarke Murphy, exhaustion.

Clarke had parachuted into a management committee off-site in Stockholm, having just come off a plane from client meetings in Latin America.

He said, "I remember thinking, 'I'm the 5:00 a.m. superhero executive, who can handle anything. I've got this."

But as the two-day meeting wore on, fatigue set in, and his usually upbeat personality started to wane. He continued:

I got in a bad mood and I hadn't realized I was bringing the whole room down. So much so that on the second day, one of my team members pulled me aside.

They said, "Murph, what is your problem? What are you angry about? Because this meeting sucks. Get a grip, start smiling, and give some positive energy. Whatever your problem is, get over it."

I was burned out. I was fried. And I hadn't realized my body language and my tone was causing people to worry. Everyone was like, "Oh, my gosh, if Clarke is in a bad mood, something is wrong with the company and he's not telling us."

For Clarke, the team member's intervention was a lightbulb moment—not only about how he showed up, but the importance of surrounding yourself with people who are willing to call you out. "I always had people around me whom I could trust and who always told me the truth," he said. "You get to know who they are and you learn to go back to them when you need a gut check on how things are going. It's about knowing who on your SLT is in it for the greater good, and not their own good."

Clarke's lightbulb stayed on for the rest of his tenure, not just in how he built and led his team, but also prompting changes to the way he managed his tightly packed schedule of travel and client commitments. "I focused so much more on prioritizing sleep and exercise. Even things like arriving at SLT meetings the day before can make a huge difference to your outlook, so you get a chance to rest and go for a run before you meet with your team."

Today, there is a big focus on vulnerability as a leader. While this is a welcome shift in the right direction, it does require balance. There is such a thing as being too vulnerable. As Jacob Morgan, speaker and bestselling author, recently told us on RRA's *Redefiners* podcast: "When you treat your organization like a big therapy session, and you don't think through 'What is it that I'm saying and why am I saying it,' you become too vulnerable."[6]

What Clarke didn't do was to unload on the team what was bothering him. He sucked it up and became the leader his team needed him to be in that moment.

The same is true for transparency. Again, this is a positive leadership trait. But just as you can be too vulnerable, you can be too much of an open book. I had one client describe his approach as radical transparency. "What does *radical* mean in this context?" I asked. His response was that it was complete and utter transparency across all aspects of the business.

"Do you mean that you will tell everyone everything, and that you want them, in turn, to tell everyone everything?" I asked.

"No," he replied.

So, I recommended a different approach, explaining that when people look for transparency, they are looking for transparency on how decisions are made, not everything a CEO knows and understands, or is thinking or feeling.

He dropped the "radical" part, and instead, focused on his belief in transparency when describing his leadership style and what was important to him.

Discuss, Debate, But You Decide

When you were part of an executive team, before becoming CEO, you would have been regularly asked to contribute to the decision-making process. Sometimes you heavily influenced the decisions and it went your way. You felt that you made the right call, that you made the decisions—but you didn't. The CEO did. Likewise, when it didn't go your way, or another decision was made, it wasn't somebody else on the team making the decision. It was the CEO.

For some executive leaders, this is frustrating. They wonder why there's not more of a consensus mindset. The team is so good; we all know our area so well, shouldn't we be making these decisions as a team? When these executives then move into a CEO role, they can sometimes hang on to that feeling. Now a CEO, they try to create what they didn't have: a democratic process where their new team is empowered to make decisions by consensus.

However, very few organizations work on consensus. It's not a good way to make decisions, nor does it reflect the accountability of the decisions.

As CEO, your role is to create the environment where the relevant leaders with the expertise, knowledge, and understanding can help *you* make the best decisions. (Clearly, you are not making all the decisions in the business, but you are making the big ones. These are the decisions I am referring to here.)

You need to establish your position early, ensuring everyone understands the rules of the game. One way of doing this is to ask your new executive team, "Do you agree that people can disagree and still commit?"

If they believe it is not possible, challenge them to think about what would happen when there isn't consensus. If they *sort of* agree, challenge them to question whether they only believe this when the decision goes their way.

The right answer is, of course, "yes." People can disagree and fully commit provided the following condition exists—that they feel they have had the opportunity to present their view and that they have been truly heard. When this happens, people can disagree with the decision and still commit 100% to the execution. However, when they feel that they were not heard, it can lead to passive aggressive behaviors and a weakened commitment to the required action.

This is not about giving "Yes I heard you" lip service to collaboration. It is a genuine exchange where you listen and understand their point of view. If you have done that, and they see that, then you can say. "Okay, Jane, I have heard your concerns, thank you. We are going to go in a different direction and here's why . . ."

One way to set up this scenario is to structure your meetings in such a way that people feel heard, while also recognizing that *you* as CEO will make the decisions. A CEO at a major bank ran a very effective version of this with his "Discuss, Debate, Decide" meeting format.

When the executive team needed to work on an important topic, the meeting was split into three parts. First, a discussion, which covered the information that people needed that was not already included in the pre-read. Second, the debate, a time when everyone got involved and the goal was to thrash out all views around the required decisions. Discourse and disagreement was encouraged. This was the opportunity to be heard, truly heard. And third, the decisions were made. The CEO made it clear that he would be the one making them. He was always happy to take counsel, but everyone understood that it was his responsibility and accountability, and it was his decision to make. Was everyone happy all the time? Of course not. But the process worked: it was engaging, it was efficient, and it created an environment for good decision-making with high commitment.

Another way to establish clarity is to articulate the specific roles people play in decision-making. Paula MacKenzie, CEO of PizzaExpress, whom we will hear more from in Chapter 9, found this necessary early in her time as CEO. "Coming into a turnaround situation, it was important that the early decisions that were being made aligned with the overall changes I felt were needed but also that people understood how they could influence them," she told me. "Members of my executive team, but even more broadly than that into the organization, had been used to making many of the decisions themselves. But some of these decisions needed to be mine."

Paula used Bain's Rapid Decision Model to help the SLT understand their roles in the process before meetings. The roles in the model are:

- **Recommend**—those who are required to make the recommendation on a course of action.
- **Agree**—those who need to agree with the final decision and whose views should be reflected in the end decision (typically functions like Legal, H&S, etc.).

- **Perform**—those who will be accountable for performing a decision once it's made.

- **Input**—those invited to provide input that may or may not be reflected in the final decision. This is the vast majority of people and is a vital part of hearing and surfacing differing perspectives.

- **Decide**—the person who will make the decision and commit the organization to action "Who is the D?"

"I had to be clear with some members that their role was not the 'Decide'; that was my role," she said. "While not everyone liked the shift, clarifying the roles upfront did stop most of the unhelpful discussions, and now I routinely hear people say, 'My input is . . .' And 'Paula (or other) is the *D* on that.'"

Beware the Hub and Spoke

Whirlpool's CEO Marc Bitzer is clear that as the new CEO, you have to be transparent about performance management. "Everybody talks about performance management, but as CEO, and especially when you are new, you need to be clear what you mean. I follow the logic: Tell me a problem earlier, it's ours. Tell me a problem late, it's yours."

But this doesn't mean that Marc always moves to solve the problem in front of him. In fact, he actively tries to avoid adopting what he calls the Hub and Spoke Model, where everyone looks to the CEO to make every decision. (Yes, CEOs have to make the big decisions, but this is not the same as making *every* decision.)

"Many CEOs, like me, are impatient, and if you give me something, I will make the decision and move on," Marc said. "But letting yourself fall into a Hub and Spoke Model ultimately creates a chimney effect. And there's only so much smoke that can go up the chimney."

He noted, "Frankly, it is still a little bit of a blind spot. Occasionally I fall back into it, and I have to fight my way back out."

Instead, Marc aims to enforce the opposite approach: The Spoke-to-Spoke Model. "If you have a problem, you need to be really clear: is that something where I need to be involved or can this and should this be dealt with spoke-to-spoke?

"The tough part is that gravity and habits pull you back in. I want to deal with some of these problems, but I need to stop myself. I will only make it worse."

Speak Last

Executives with a seat at the senior leadership table are expected to provide a view on the issues affecting the business. They can fire out their perspective at varying times in meetings, group sessions, and even in the corridors. They give their opinion because they have one. Some executives fall into the trap of giving their opinion too early. Some do this intentionally, to set their position, and to try and influence any other members who haven't yet fully formed their view. Often, they want other people to share their view so they can get things done the way they want them (or how they think is best for the organization).

You can't do that as CEO. Your view is too influential.

If you, as CEO, lead a discussion with your view, you have effectively led the witness and what you will get back will be strangely close to what you already thought. Fancy that. This is the comically depicted example of a CEO entering a room and saying, "We are here to discuss the problem of X, I think we should do Y, but I am *really* interested in hearing your views."

It can sometimes be difficult to not fall victim to speaking first, or "setting the scene." You can't have the room sitting in silence, so you feel, as CEO, you need to lead. You start the discussion, but often in doing so, you have also finished it.

When Nelson Mandela was asked how he became such a good leader, he simply said: "Because I learned to speak last."

It's great leadership to avoid leading the conversation or giving your view early, but it is also rare. So, you need to explain what you are doing and why. Otherwise, people might see it as a lack of interest or some sort of test.

One version I heard recently (and offered correction on) was, "I'm not going the start the discussion; I have a view and will share it at the end, but first I want to hear what you all think." In other words, I know the answer and I just want to see if you are smart enough to see it; let's play a guess-what-I-am-thinking game. This will not produce a meeting conducive to sharing and challenging towards better understanding and the best decision.

A CEO I advised, who was a long-time COO and regional leader, found that speaking last was a massive shift in his leadership style. He was highly regarded as the person who got things done and solved problems. People came to him with their challenges, and he dealt with them quickly.

He was used to having an opinion and sharing it—and when he became CEO, it only became worse.

Now he had to move even faster, and he had even more problems to fix. His time was compressed, and he wanted to perform. He would move from back-to-back meetings, impatiently laying down solution after solution. If someone disagreed, he would rise to the debate, regularly winning. It took some time and very direct stakeholder feedback for him to realize that this was not good leadership.

"What is your role in these meetings?" I asked

"To make the decision," he said

"Yes, but is it the decision or *the best decision*?" I pushed.

"Of course, the best decisions," he replied.

"Your role," I suggested, "is to create an environment in these meetings where the people you have in these teams are comfortable to share their views and opinions, tangible and intangible, so that you can collect all of that data and then make the *best decision*. When you start with your summation of the problem and your choice of solution, you stop that from happening. You are absolutely leading the witness. You might as well not have the meeting at all. Just send them an email telling them what you have decided."

"But they need to feel part of the process," he replied.

"Well, this is not achieving that. All it is doing is wasting their time. They are not even learning because you don't show your working," I pointed out.

He nodded. I could see he was about to say it, so before he did, I said, "I know that most of the time you *are* right. I get that. I also get that you are in a hurry and don't want to waste time."

"It's true, most of the time I am 85 to 90% right!" he said with a good amount of genuine humility and some frustration.

I smiled with agreement, before adding, "One of the differences between being a COO and a CEO is that that being 10% wrong on a decision as COO is something you can live with, but as CEO, it might not be. It is like flying a plane from Sydney to LA—at the start, being off 10% makes little difference, but if you don't correct it, you won't land in LA, you'll land in Mexico City. The opportunity to hear from the people you have in these roles is that 10% margin of error. It matters. Speak last."

Showing Your Working

"Showing your working" is a concept I use with leaders to explain the importance of explaining their thinking as a development tool. Think of a mathematics exam—you can get the answer right and still not get full marks because you didn't show how you arrived at it. It is similar with leading people, you can have the right answer, but the real uplift comes when you share how you got to the right answer so people can replicate the process.

The New CEO Checklist

- **Think first team.** Establish the right team dynamics from the start. Your SLT members need to see each other as their first team. If they don't, you'll quickly be hamstrung by a team that is too busy protecting its respective function to support your strategic vision.

- **Don't strive for absolute harmony.** Just as important as finding the right people is ensuring they work together as a high-performing team. Strive for productive tension. And don't forget that team dynamics will need constant development and prioritization.

- **Harness the diversity of your SLT.** The best top teams bring a mosaic of different personalities, experiences, and skill sets. You will need to flex your approach and overcome your functional bias to unlock this potential.

- **Personal habits matter.** The way you show up is critical to fostering the right behaviors and mindsets, not only across the wider organization, but also your SLT. Don't fall into the trap of thinking you're superhuman—get enough sleep and exercise, so you can lead clearly and consistently.

- **Make the right decisions.** Know the difference between the decisions that *you* have to make as CEO and the decisions that your SLT can (and should) be making without you. You are responsible for the big, strategic decisions. For most other decisions, empower your team to work together to make them.

CHAPTER 9

Working with the Board

"You can do what I cannot do. I can do what you cannot do. Together we can achieve great things."

—Mother Theresa

A unique aspect of being a CEO is working with (and for) a board of directors. If this is your first CEO role, you will be in new territory.

As a senior executive, you may have interacted with the board—when you're in the C-suite, having time on the board agenda is often a sign of progression and responsibility. Perhaps you had the chance to present, address certain questions, or even participate in committees and projects.

If you were hired internally, you will have likely had the opportunity to engage with the directors and chair you'll now work with as CEO.

Opportunities like these give you a decent insight into board interactions and the start of a relationship with the chair and directors, but do not assume that you'll enjoy a similar homecoming now that you are CEO.

When you present as a C-suite executive, you are in a *show role*, and generally very well prepared. Most boards are gentle on visiting executives and leave the tough aspects for the sitting CEO. The board dynamic also shifts in the presence of incomers.

It is common for first-time CEOs to find that they have greatly underestimated the time it takes to manage the board interactions and demands. They find that being in board meetings is often taxing, and navigating the different roles and personalities a challenge. For many, they had thought that being a CEO meant they were in charge—now they find answering to the board more than a little disempowering.

This may not be your experience. If it is, however, you are not alone.

One transition regret that is shared regularly by new CEOs is that they wished they had better used the board in their first couple of years. Over time, they get a better sense of what the board can deliver and realize that, for a variety of reasons, they did not engage the board in the most effective way early on.

PepsiCo's CEO Ramon Laguarta is one CEO who didn't fall into this trap. He was clear early on that he needed to focus on the board and made an intentional effort to spend quality time with directors, even though he'd already been exposed to many of them during the 20-plus years he'd been with the company. "I visited them for a day, or even in some cases two days," he told me. "I tried to create a personal relationship and the space for them to tell me what they really thought about the business."

For Ramon, there was a clear benefit of engaging the board early: securing alignment around his vision for PepsiCo to become *the* global leader in beverages and convenience food. "I wanted to reset; I wanted to change some key things, and I needed their support," he candidly told me. "I tried to establish a level of trust with them. I didn't just tell them the positives. I was also open about our vulnerabilities, the full picture."

That's not to say that the discussions were not without challenges. Some directors took longer to align on how to pivot the company toward growth. "I had to get their acceptance to double our capital expenditure and really increase our investments behind the brands. They trusted me, but in the first 12 months they were still a bit like, 'Show me the money.'"

(Incidentally, Ramon went on to tell me that for the past five years he's been in office, PepsiCo has been the fastest-growing, large-scale, global consumer goods company.)

Today, he continues to spend one-on-one time with directors, visiting half of the board's members each year for a day or two. He turns to them for advice—for both himself and some of his management team—and involves them in interview processes and the development of his top team, as well as some of the up-and-coming leaders whom he thinks could one day take over the CEO reigns.

For Ramon, the board's role is not just about governance. It's there to help him navigate the strategic topics. And the upshot? "They are there to call when I have a problem," he smiled.

Strategic Asset or Necessary Evil?

It can be useful to check your own perceptions about the role you think a board should play: is it a necessary evil or a strategic asset? Assuming you don't have a problematic board, this is largely a choice that *you* must make.

The giveaway that a CEO perceives the board as a necessary evil is when board meetings are highly orchestrated and highly controlled, with overly prepared, scripted, and rehearsed presentations: one-way information devoid of opportunities for discussion. Yes, you need to present information, but you should do so in a way and as a means of extracting the greatest amount of wisdom, experience, and value from the board.

When the board is seen as a strategic asset, CEOs often take a deliberate approach to creating space for the board to contribute in more meaningful and substantive ways, especially around strategy. It is not the board's responsibility to create the strategy, but its input can be extremely additive to the CEO's and SLT's thinking. The speed of change is such that strategy is no longer a topic you cover once a year at some tropical paradise.

Use pre-reads effectively and set up topics in board meetings with minimal amount of presentation and maximum amount of discussion. Use the board as a sparring partner.

If your view is that the board is a necessary evil, I encourage you to work on changing your perspective. That will likely mean rethinking the way you approach and interact with the board, but it might also mean pushing to change some of the members. Ultimately, your board should be a strategic asset.

Get to Know Them Individually

Many of us have only had one boss at any given time during our careers. Now, as CEO, you have several bosses—and these bosses come and go. This is a significant shift and one that new CEOs often find a challenge.

Your board is a collection of individuals, often with long and varied work experiences. Like any stakeholder, there is benefit to investing time and effort in building effective relationships—just as PepsiCo's Ramon understands. This is your responsibility. Directors (the chair will be different) will often follow your lead, so if you don't make the effort, they may believe that is your preference and will likely give you space.

Take time to understand individual director's views on the company, culture, top team, and opportunities, as well as what they believe the board's role is for the organization—and how the relationship with the CEO should work. Treat them as a group of individuals, rather than as a single group with a fixed identity. Make the effort to go to them, to meet their time availability, and ensure that you set the relationships up well from the outset.

Around a month before becoming CEO at Whirlpool, Marc Bitzer visited around four directors at their respective homes "to break the ice." "These directors all had CEO experience, so I asked them all the same question, "How did you prepare yourself? What did you do first and why?"

Today, he has calls scheduled between every board meeting with the lead director and committee chairs. For the other directors, he reaches out twice a year. "The calls are ad hoc and have no specific agenda," he said. "I just want to hear what they have to say, what they are worried about, and whether there were agenda items missing from the meetings." Marc also noted, "It's critical because the board meetings are, to an extent, formal. The real discussion happens in the hallway."

It can often take the first year or so to find a workable rhythm with the board. This includes forming the right relationships and establishing the "right to lead"—the shared understanding of where you and the board start and stop, and building the situational trust to do so with autonomy. Being too accommodating or tolerating ambiguous boundaries early on may set you up for trouble in the future—especially if you allow yourself to be easily overruled.

CEO/Chair Relationship

Three months after Mark Clouse became Campbell's CEO, Keith R. McLoughlin became chair of the board. McLoughlin had been on the board since 2016 and served as Campbell's interim CEO from May 2018 until Mark took the helm in January 2019. Mark describes it as a "watershed moment." "I could not have had a better partner because his real superpower is self-awareness," he told me. "He had a firm grasp on the issues at the company and knows exactly where his strengths are and where he doesn't have expertise. We work extremely well together because of the complementary nature of our experiences—and I believe we're very effective."

All members of the board are not equal. The chair is by far the most important member for you as CEO. Your relationship with the chair will be a strong influencer of your success as CEO, and in turn, the organization.

In the past, this relationship has been one of mentor and mentee—the chair would regularly have much broader experience than the CEO. A version of "old heads on young shoulders."

While there are still many examples of this dynamic, it is far more common that the CEO has an equal amount of commercial experience as the chair. In these cases, there is a great opportunity to work closely, while also respecting each other's roles and subsequent responsibilities.

This relationship will need to be a key focus for you from the earliest interview through your entire tenure. Setting it up well is very important.

Sometimes this means moving quickly to align expectations. Lyssa McGowan at Pets at Home, for example, sat down with her chair to discuss their working relationship before she'd even started the role. "He is a long-standing chair, who has coached several new CEOs," she told me. "He'd put together a really helpful document based on his experience about how we could work together. One important element was how we could avoid treading on each other's toes. I told him, 'That's great, but truly, there is a lot that I don't know—it's my first CEO role. Please don't worry about treading on my toes. I'm not defensive. I'm up for anything you can do to be helpful, so don't hold back. Just step in. Tell me what you think.' And he absolutely has—which has been incredibly helpful."

When in Doubt, Share

I discussed transparency as a positive leadership attribute earlier in Chapter 8. The benefit extends to how you work with your board. For many CEOs, it is the *only* way to work with the board.

Mark Clouse, took on Campbell's CEO role when the organization was not performing well, and needed a massive business and cultural turnaround. High on his list of priorities was rebuilding trust with the board. "There was an opportunity to significantly improve management's trust of the board and the board's trust of management," he told me.

His approach was to get the board "deeply immersed in the business" and to be completely transparent. "My belief was that I could improve trust quickly if I demystified the good, the bad, and the ugly," he said. "This wasn't about managing the messaging. This was about getting everybody in the boat together."

This turned out to be a shock to the system—for both the board and the executive team. "The board wasn't used to getting into that level of detail. And at first, it was a fairly dramatic change for both the board and management. But we pushed through this because I knew we would never overcome this lack of trust until we all got onto the same page. It was one of the most important things I did early on and something that I would absolutely do again."

Lyssa McGowan took a similar approach with dealing with her board of directors after becoming CEO of Pets at Home. She'd been on another board before as a non-executive director (NED) and had seen the CEO keep information and the board at arm's length. From this vantage point, she was clear that she would take the opposite approach, pulling the board close. "I was a completely open book, very transparent, and candid," she said. "I would find space outside of board meetings to talk about what they think. I took the view that these were very smart people who were being paid to help."

She told the board, in no uncertain terms, that she would tell them everything, that nothing was out of bounds—and that she had her own expectations in return. "I told them, 'You can ask me any question and you will get the truth, even when you might not like the answer. But the quid pro quo is that you need to be helpful and engaged and not ask those annoying NED questions, the ones where you don't really need to know the answer.' This really set the tone and they have been a huge support over my first 18 months."

Being transparent with the board is good practice and enhances its ability to be a strategic asset. When in doubt, share.

Boards Are Time-Consuming

In RRA's research of nearly 200 new CEOs, most said that they spent 25% of their time with the board or on board-related activities.[1]

For 44% of new CEOs, this was more time than they had expected or planned for going into the role. For 42%, it matched their expectations.

The takeaway is that as you plan your transition, allow for up to 25% of your time (and maybe a greater percentage of your energy) to go to the board. Consider this in terms of your stated and unstated expectations of how much time you will have for the things you will want to do.

Common Mistakes with the Board

Working effectively with your board of directors is a critical factor not only in your transition, but over the longer period of your time as CEO. While there are potentially many areas where the CEO/board relationship can get strained, the following are some more commonly made mistakes to avoid.

Trying to Manage the Board

Some CEOs wrongly assume that becoming CEO means that they are the ultimate authority, finally in charge. Not quite true. These same CEOs can also sometimes wrongly assume that part of their sphere of control includes the board. There are numerous stories of CEOs who worked hard to select, direct, and manage directors in order to increase control. These stories are not held up in a positive light.

Many CEOs who try to manage the board are quickly reminded that this is not the dynamic—you do not manage the board.

The board is a group unlike any other in your organization and while it can be influenced and "sold," it is designed to not bow down to your office. Its purpose is to challenge you, challenge your thinking, and challenge your team. It represents (and serves) the shareholders—the board's fiduciary responsibility is to them. Everything it does should be in the best service of the shareholders' investments, returns, and betterment. The board wants to help you and the organization succeed as long as those things are not mutually exclusive.

As Whirlpool's Marc Bitzer told me, "No matter what you think and no matter how you feel, you serve the board. No CEO is bigger than the board."

Avoiding the Board

There is so much to do when you become CEO that it can be a challenge to prioritize your actions. The noise from employees below you in the organization will often be far louder than that coming above, from the board. However, one of the worst things you can do is ignore or avoid the board "while you get on top of other important things."

Ideally, you will have had a chance to start to form relationships with the board through your selection process. Make the directors a priority early in your tenure. Without their support you will not have a very long run at the top of the house.

"Overcommunicate is probably the simplest way to describe it," explained one CEO I interviewed. "I talk to the chair at least once a week, sometimes more. I try hard to listen to feedback on how they want to receive information. Some boards say, "Keep me out of the weeds." Others want more detail. It's up to you to manage that proactively."

Not Understanding the Board's Role and Yours

In many organizations, the distinction between the CEO role and the board's role is far from crystal clear. In some cases, it's downright opaque. I have seen situations where the CEO had full support from the board, and others where the CEO title should have been general manager. There are many different possibilities, and you often do not know which one you'll face until after you start.

Ultimately, you need to understand the scope and role of the board and what makes a board effective. Your board has three primary functions: hire (and fire) the CEO, approve the strategy, and manage risk via various governance committees.

Directors are absolutely responsible for your appointment and performance management. In fact, a CEO transition is one of, if not *the* biggest, challenge and measure of success that a board, and specifically the chair, can face. The decision to select you, and to keep you, is at the very top of the list of board responsibilities. Your CEO transition can be as stressful for the chair and the Nomination Committee, as it is for you.

There are gray areas, however. Designing versus approving the strategy is one. In my experience, the right answer is that the board approves the strategy; it does not set it. However, I have seen many boards overstep the mark in terms of strategy, especially when it is a new and/or first-time CEO. This is one of the areas where you need to be really clear from the start (actually from the interview stage). Boards don't set strategy—CEOs do.

If your board disagrees, then you have a challenge. This is often seen with more inexperienced directors, who are either current or recent CEOs themselves, and who find it difficult to stop calling the shots. Yet you can also find dominant chairs who feel it is their role to run the organization.

Get a read on your directors and chair early and try to understand how they see their roles. This is something experienced CEOs tend to do well—they are clear about the role of the board from the onset, even if the board is not. Experienced CEOs set the boundaries very early on and work to make sure that the board—both as a collective and a set of individuals—also understands and respects them. They have learned (often the hard way) that if you don't set the expectations, the board will.

A commonly cited phrase is that good boards should be noses in, but hands out. Conceptually this is true: directors should understand what is happening, what decisions are forming, and what challenges lie ahead of the organization, while leaving the running of the business to you and your SLT. Naturally, the caveat here is "good boards."

Should you luck out with an effective and fully functional board, then your transition will have a greatly improved chance of going smoothly. What is more likely is that you will find a mix of function and dysfunction along with a mix of quality both in terms of the directors' capabilities, and their motivations and agendas.

Early discussions with the chair and board on how you will work together, how you will disagree, how you will manage conflict, and how you will deal with difficult events are very valuable. Resist the temptation to get into the content immediately. Spend some time early on talking about how you will manage your respective responsibilities and relationships.

Not Realizing That You Are One of the Board's Key Risks

Part of your job is to help the board deliver on its fiduciary and governance responsibilities. For this reason, understanding risk management from a board's perspective is invaluable. If you can think like the board around the risk areas that impact the organization and you, as CEO, it will greatly help your relationship dynamic.

You consider risks every day—it is a key tenet of your role and one of your ultimate responsibilities. The risk you probably don't consider enough is you.

Great CEOs regularly consider the risk of their own health and mortality, and they have firm succession plans in place at all times (in fact, the best time to start succession planning is your first day as the new CEO).

The board will have a wider view of risks that relate to you: your decision-making, your motivations, your biases, your character, your integrity, your relationships, your past.

You are one of key risks to the organization and the board is responsible for mitigating it.

Understanding and appreciating this will help you to tailor your communication to the board, as well as balance your response to questions that seek to uncover any impending risk you might pose. Don't take it personally; they are doing their jobs.

Getting Too Familiar

The chair and directors are not your friends. They are responsible for the governance of the organization and your performance. Yes, they can be friendly, and you can develop a close relationship, but they are not your friends. Don't get too familiar. Give them the deference they deserve.

One way overfamiliarity can show up is being underprepared for board meetings—or worse, when you start ideating on the fly. It can also show up if you do not keep the board, and importantly the chair, aware of what you'll be discussing at each meeting. The board will listen to what you say and they will take it seriously. It is not an environment where you can say, "Just ignore that I said that," or, "Let's just forget I brought that up." Just as you know not to joke with airport security, be careful with your board, especially early on.

In the stakeholder feedback I received for one CEO, the chair told me how the CEO had announced that she was going to cancel a significant capital expenditure project. Two of the directors, who were sponsors of the project, had reacted badly, completely derailing the meeting. Afterward, the directors had said they were disappointed in the chair for letting the CEO's plans get to that point without the board knowing.

"What the CEO should have done, and needs to do, is discuss these things with me before the meeting," the chair explained. "To be supportive of her, and to run an effective meeting, I need to know what is going to be raised or introduced. In this case, I would have guessed the directors' reactions and could have prepared them ahead of the meeting. It would have allowed for a discussion of the merits of the project. Instead, the directors convinced the board to reject the decision and force the CEO to come back with a solid business case for why the project should be cancelled. It knocked her confidence and affected the board dynamic for the next couple of meetings."

The other issues than can manifest with overfamiliarity is your lack of support for your SLT when they are presenting. You are relaxed and comfortable, so you think they should be as well—it's only the board, after all. Remember that presenting to a board is a key area of development for executives as they get more senior, and it can be anxiety-provoking. Your job here is to make sure you are setting them up for success every time they interact with the board.

Assuming Silence Is Approval

Many new CEOs assume that a silent board means a job well done. Yes and no. There is a fine line between being too involved and too absent. As CEO, you need the board's engagement, interest, and challenge in order to make the best decisions for the organization. Without that, you lose a valuable set of inputs that are built into your organizational design in order to benefit you.

Many directors are very experienced in both their role and in their previous roles as senior executives, or even CEOs. Often, when you are a new CEO, experienced directors give you space, give you time. They step back and allow you to find your feet, to explore the organization, and start to form your own impressions. They stay silent.

I have seen CEOs early on not recognize this, and instead, take the lack of comment, direction, or intervention as a glowing endorsement of their brilliance. This is typically not the case. You need to engage the board early, you need to encourage the discussions that will ultimately help you, and you need to go to them and prompt the right discussions.

Silence is not necessarily endorsement. It could be the opposite. Make sure you know either way.

The PE Factor

Your ownership structure (and its knock-on effect on the composition and behavior of the board) will impact your approach, speed, and freedom to operate. Leading a public company is considered by most to be the clearest to understand and operate within. But what if you are the new CEO in a private-equity-owned (PE-owned) business or a family-owned business? Then the rules of the game are quite different.

Paula MacKenzie has the vantage point of sitting on both public company boards and being CEO of a PE-backed business—PizzaExpress, a major restaurant chain that was acquired in 2014 for $1.54 billion and then underwent a restructuring deal by two different PE firms in 2020, two years before Paula took on the role. She is clear that listed boards are looking at a much longer time horizon when driving results.

She said, "Directors on a listed board represent a broad group of shareholders which can be constantly changing. When you are owned by private equity, the directors are focused on value creation within a defined period of time. So, you need to know where in that cycle of value creation you are because that determines whether you've got six months or five years to deliver. Knowing that is essential, as is understanding the investment thesis in detail."

But she is clear that different PE houses have different approaches, and "seeing one does not mean you have seen them all."

"You need to get under the skin of who your PE backers are. In my case, I have two and they are working entirely differently in terms of their time horizons, intrusiveness, and empowerment."

She continued, "The surprise I found was that they don't really care what I planned to do, just when the results would be delivered. I found that strange that there was no interest or excitement in what I was doing, and at first, I thought that maybe I wasn't communicating it clearly or not being exciting enough, but they just weren't interested."

"Because they don't care about the inputs, they don't give you feedback or support like you get from a listed board. This can make the role feel even lonelier," she added.

There are similarities when you are CEO of a family-owned or family-controlled business. Even if the families' wealth is controlled by a trust, you may still get family members on the board who feel that they have more right to assert themselves. Understanding the governance structure with family-owned businesses is very important (as well as adherence to it, i.e., whether they work within the structure or work around it).

Board Conflicts

In my research, 63% of new CEOs said that they had experienced a significant conflict with their respective boards in their first 12 months. The most common areas were around strategy and the style or contribution of the chair.[2]

This is not to say that this is a negative aspect of your role. In most cases, the conflict can be resolved and both parties move forward. I am raising this because it's important to have a balanced expectation going in that it may not be all clear sailing.

One example was a second-time CEO who had recurring style conflicts with the chair. "He is a brilliant chair of the company and a really good and effective mentor to me, but he was quite a poor chair of board meetings," he told me. "He had this very unusual style where he viewed the role of the chair as being a kind of protagonist-in-chief, rather than facilitator of the discussion. That created frustration for other board members who didn't feel they got enough air time to share their views or had their views pre-positioned by the chair before they got the chance."

Another CEO had an early board conflict over the budgeting process. He shared how the previous CEO had had a difficult relationship with the board and everything had turned into a "hostile negotiation between the board and the management." "The mistake I made as the incoming new CEO was to trust the CFO to do the budgeting process the way he and his team had always done it," he told me. "It was like a game of hide and seek: here are the numbers but they are not the real numbers."

The new CEO decided to notify the board about the situation, which he said not only damaged the CFO's credibility, but his own, too. "As a reaction, the board asked me to review previous years' budgets," he said. "It was an important lesson in how not to deal with the board. The result was increased oversight and involvement, which caused friction in other areas for the next several months while I reestablished their trust in the numbers."

While you might not be able to avoid a conflict altogether, it's often a good idea to use your early meetings with directors to discuss how you will deal with them should they arise. Doing so, will go a long way to helping you overcome disagreements or misalignments when the time comes.

The Board's Concerns of You, Their New CEO

Which concerns do boards most commonly raise with me when discussing their new CEO? One is that their new CEO is acting like a COO—and enjoying it. Another is wondering when the CEO has time to actually think about the business, given how busy they appear to be.

A CEO behaving like a great COO is a real concern, especially when you are a first-time CEO. The question the board (and sometimes the SLT) asks is, "Will this person ever be able to distance themselves from the doing, enough to truly lead the organization, or have we made the mistake of hiring an execution specialist into the CEO role?"

When you are new to role, your desire to be effective is strongest, and that means you are often involved in more than you should be. You are learning things, questioning things, and fixing things. The challenge is that you can get stuck in the doing, in the execution, and being too *operational*. You see so many things that need fixing and keep telling yourself that if you can just fix this *last thing*, you will be able to step back and start to do the CEO role.

It is normal to roll up your sleeves early and get things done. However, it's important to make sure you are clear in your communication to the board and the business that this is a short-term approach—and be disciplined about that. It is very hard to be able to see the longer-term opportunities and challenges if you are knee-deep in execution, operations, meetings, and projects.

The board will wait and be patient with you, but don't miss the point that they will be concerned that this will end up being your *modus operandi* longer term. Make it clear that you understand the role. Tell them how long you expect to be operational and keep them updated. Watch that you don't get used to it or addicted to the dopamine hit of fixing things yourself.

A crucial part of your role is thinking about the organization 5 to 10 years from now. You are the only person who truly has this responsibility and the only one who has the perspective to be able to do it effectively. You are the organization's chief steward. You need to make time for this responsibility— and that time needs to be clearly allocated.

It is not good enough to say to the board that you focus on your long-term vision on weekends or around your other appointments. If your diary is back-to-back every day, you are signalling to the board that you are not spending enough time *thinking about the business*.

Explain your scheduling to them. Tell them when you have your thinking time. Leave some gaps in your calendar. Think about working toward 10% to 20% of your diary being unallocated. This indicates to the board that you are moving out of the doing stage of transition and into the real aspects of being an effective CEO.

Can I Have That in Writing?

Unfortunately, this advice might be too late for you, depending on where you are in your transition process. The concept of pre-contracting is something that I hear commonly from second-time CEOs who have reflected on their first-time experiences and now fully understand the opportunity you have before you start to contract your scope and authority with the board.

You might remember Hans Vestberg, the CEO of Verizon, from Chapter 2, who walked the board through his white paper *before* accepting the role. This is perfect pre-contracting—a chance to address upfront the challenges that may occur as you drive the changes you feel the organization needs to be successful, and dealing with the *"when, not if"* before it becomes something that derails your progress.

After 10 years leading a global company, a successful CEO decided to accept an offer to run a larger, more complex organization in the same industry. It was a big decision to leave his existing organization, which had prospered under his leadership. But coming in as a second-time CEO had afforded him lessons on how to set himself up for success.

One of his biggest learnings was around the impact that an effective board would have on his ability to be successful and drive the change that the organization needed. The

CEO's new organization was the result of a merger, and still had very high levels of family ownership. In the discussions that took place before he accepted the role, it was clear that the board needed a new chair and that one of the directors was causing issues on the board. Some had referred to this individual as a "board meeting terrorist." The CEO made it a key criteria for accepting the role that the chair was changed and that there was an immediate plan to deal with the negative director. Forewarned was forearmed.

First-time CEOs either assume that they will be able to act freely, or they lack the confidence to ask questions before they take the job, instead opting to deal with it once they're through the door. More experienced CEOs have often learned the hard way that it makes more sense to do it sooner, rather than later. They will often have discussions with the board during the recruitment process to not only seek alignment on scenarios that often cause conflict, but also to establish their right to lead. Examples are:

- When (not if) I want to change out an Exco member that the board thinks should stay—what happens? Will I have the freedom to make the change?

- If I determine that a business that the board has previously supported is not core to our strategy moving forward, will you block my ability to sell it?

Establishing ground rules at the outset helps build a constructive alliance between you and the board. Remember, boards can often be risk- and change-averse and directors will worry that you, as new CEO, will make changes that create significant instability, especially with the people they know. Be mindful of this.

Dealing with the Street

Alongside dealing with the board, interacting with investors will be another learning curve as you transition into the CEO role (i.e., unless you've already been a Chief Investment Officer or CFO in a listed business). A stakeholder group unlike any other, investors can create a significant amount of work for you—and stress.

This was something that Mark Clouse was well aware of, having previously been CEO at Pinnacle before joining Campbell's. "When I got to Pinnacle, I hadn't realized how much of my time would be committed to engaging the street and communicating with investors," he told me. "So, by the time I joined Campbell's, I was familiar with the time constraints I'd face and the reporting that was required to maintain investor relationships."

Not all new CEOs enjoy this luxury. Just as it's easy to underestimate the time you need to deal with the board, many new CEOs soon find they've also underestimated how much time and work goes into managing the investor community—and preparing for meetings.

As one CEO told me, "There's no end in terms of how much prep you could do for a call." He said, "Sometimes you get questions that are down the middle of the fairway and your prep can feel wasted. But every so often, we got a very specific line of questioning and the prep saved me. You need to strike your own balance of knowing when enough prep is enough."

Some new CEOs find themselves in front of investors early on as the timing of their arrival coincides with pre-planned quarterly updates. Even when this is not the case, many new CEOs still make it a priority to have meetings with the major investors and analysts in the first weeks of starting (if not before starting).

For many CEOs, their approach with investors mirrors that of the board. Those who took the view of transparency with the board, took a similar approach with their investors.

One CEO found they had their first earning call within two weeks of starting. "I was clear from the outset that there was a lot of wood to chop to transform the business and luckily it didn't upset the guidance," he said. "Then, after the first three months we had a capital market's day, and I did a massive reset of expectations. Fortunately, again there was limited change in the guidance. It was the transparency upfront that was crucial."

However, what many, including PepsiCo's Ramon Laguarta, learn quickly is that the investors are a tougher audience to work with and that the level and type of engagement differs. "I always felt more uncomfortable with the investors than the board because no one can fully prepare you at the start about exactly what engaging with the investor community will be like," he said. "The rules are complex. You want to be transparent and build trust while recognizing you are dealing with external parties."

Ramon added, "I didn't feel very comfortable at the beginning, I must say. It's hard to get the equation right. Over time, you learn and it becomes much simpler. But I remember the first earnings calls were very stressful for me."

My advice is to do your homework. Identify the most vocal analysts and investors who join calls. Understand "hot button" issues that may come up—and prepare for them. And practice, practice, practice. Your tone and language matter. Ultimately, the more you do it, the better you will become.

The New CEO Checklist

- **Engage the board early.** Your board is a strategic asset. Investing time at the start of your transition will pay dividends. Don't get so distracted by the noise from the lower levels of the organization that you forget to look upward.

- **Clarity counts.** Take the lead to understand the board's expectations of you early on and seek alignment around your vision—ideally, before accepting the CEO role. Establish appropriate boundaries from the start. Ambiguity will only trip you up further down the road.

- **Forge deep relationships.** Your relationship with the chair can make or break your success as CEO. It pays to forge a good relationship with them. But don't overlook your individual directors. You'll also need to spend significant time getting to know them individually.

- **Establish a relationship based on transparency.** Being transparent with the board is good practice and enhances the ability of directors to be a strategic asset. Adopt the rule of when in doubt, share.

CHAPTER 10

Shaping the Culture

"Your culture can never be good enough."
—Doug Mack, former CEO, Fanatics

Remember Stephanie Tully, who appears in other chapters of this book. She joined Jetstar at perhaps the most challenging time in the budget airline's 20-year history. It was November 2022, just nine months after Australia had officially reopened its borders following the worst of the Covid-19 pandemic. Like many industries the world over, Australia's airline sector was slowly coming out of hibernation—having lost $19 billion in revenues between 2018 and 2019/20.[1]

At the time, Jetstar had earned the unenviable title of the country's most unreliable airline, as operational headaches and supply chain issues led to delays and cancellations that drew the wrath of both customers and the media. "We were on the front page of newspapers most days and it became a bit of a joke for the country to be honest," she told me. "There was a real focus from the board and management team for me to hurry up and fix it."

When I met with Stephanie, she was heading toward her first-year anniversary as Jetstar's CEO. She'd spent much of her early transition working with the team to move fast to reboot Jetstar's operational performance, while also trying to get to grips with improving the airline's culture and customer experience—something she cared and knew deeply about, having previously been Chief Customer Officer at Qantas, Jetstar's more premium parent airline.

One of the first things that Stephanie noticed was that, while she was flying with Jetstar, her executive team weren't flying Jetstar as regularly. She immediately put it into senior leaders' and executives' role requirements that they must fly Jetstar at least 50% of the time.

"Cultures are changed one conversation at a time, so for me it was an obvious decision," she said. "Every time I fly with Jetstar, I get to spend time with four or five cabin crew and two pilots. It meant I was getting better information than my executive team about what was going on. It became a bit embarrassing that their new CEO knew how things were working better than anyone else."

Stephanie went a step further, making a point of not just being a passenger on Jetstar flights, but an active member of the crew. Once the plane lands, she stands at the front to say goodbye to the passengers, and then spends time with the crew to tidy the plane and fold the seatbelts back to their original position.

"It's not a major effort but it says to the crew that you're a normal person, that you're listening, and that you care," she told me. "The cabin crew are also the grapevine of the business, so it has a huge effect. If I sit in the cockpit for flights, within a few hours of us landing, 200 pilots know about it."

Making it clear from Day One that flying Jetstar was a requirement for all executives set the tone for Stephanie's leadership and for the culture she wanted to build. (When we spoke, she mentioned that Vanessa Hudson, the new CEO of Qantas, was about to fly Jetstar for her first board meeting next month.)

For Stephanie, reigniting Jetstar's culture meant encouraging the company to get back to its roots as the younger, hungrier brand than its parent company Qantas. "We called it Program DNA because, at its heart, the Jetstar brand is all about energy and a passion for transformation. These qualities had gone missing over the years, so I challenged the leadership team to go back to our core DNA, telling them, 'As the younger, challenger brand we can get creative and be hungry to try more stuff.'"

The rallying cry for the leadership team and organization was its Every Dollar Counts, Every Minute Matters campaign—an effort to remind people about the fundamentals of Jetstar's business model (where both for Jetstar's customers and its people, reliability and a low-cost focus is critical) and the purpose of the company in Australian's lives. "It doesn't engage people to talk about why Jetstar needs to have a 15% profit margin," Stephanie said. "It engages people to say Jetstar has this incredibly unique role in Australian culture, where it has democratized travel."

Stephanie continued, "Without Jetstar, lots of people would never get on a plane because they wouldn't be able to afford it. Every dollar counts for our customers because they're often flying once a year and have worked bloody hard to be able to afford it."

To that end, Stephanie has publicly apologized to "everyone we've let down in our 20-year history." She also brought in a new executive team member to focus on transformation.

It's early days, but Stephanie says Every Dollar Counts, Every Minute Matters gave the company a framework about what it needed to chase—and what needed to change to get there. It also led to a more performance-driven culture.

"The airline industry was coming back from three years of hibernation, where the whole paradigm of travel had changed. A lot of people opted out of the industry, so you've not only got a new CEO, but you've got an incredible amount of new people and operational chaos," Stephanie said. She added:

> *I'd have one-to-ones with my leadership team where I would explain what I thought had lacked in the business, and there were a couple of times when some people felt that I was being too focused on what had gone wrong. But I guess what you've got to come back to is: what's your job as CEO? My job is to be the CEO of this business and leave it in better shape than I found it. It's about getting people to love working for it and customers to at least not hate it, and ideally love it. So, sitting in this business and patting everyone on the back is not going to get us there."*

Assessing Your Culture

As CEO, you are ultimately responsible for the culture of your organization. As its most senior leader, you will set the standard for the behaviors and values that everyone else emulates. As the saying goes, "You will get what you are prepared to ignore." In other words, if you accept poor behavior, then expect that to become the norm, not an outlier.

We define *culture* as "the shared set of assumptions held by people within an organization about who we choose to hire, how we behave, how we lead, what we reward and what we punish."[2]

As my colleague Gretchen Anderson, who leads RRA's culture advisory offering, explained, culture includes the tone set by leadership at the top of the organization—not just what leaders say, but what they do. And it includes the echo from the bottom—the beliefs and actions that are held and demonstrated broadly across the enterprise. "Culture is the difference between an organization chart that makes sense on paper, and the way that work really gets done," she said.[3]

When you're new to the CEO role, you will need to first assess your organization's culture and then decide what you want it to be. Changing your culture is difficult and takes time. Do not shy away from the task. Start early and recognize that you are leading the change in everything you do—like Stephanie did by flying Jetstar or folding the seatbelts with the crew.

At the time of writing, the culture topic most of my clients are grappling with is how to handle the "new normal" of hybrid working/return to the office—something where the needs of companies are colliding head-on with the wants of many employees.

The tumult of the last few years—multiple waves of the Covid-19 pandemic, geopolitical uncertainty, increased social unrest, and the recent bleak economic outlook—has taken its toll on people and performance. The entire contract between workers and institutions is being re-written, with workers walking away from roles at historically high rates.

Like all CEOs, and their boards, you will want to know if you have a *good culture*. It is not a simple answer. Cultures are complex systems. Leaders can understand and control the *tone at the top,* but the *echo from the bottom* is much more elusive because standard surveys often lack nuance and fail to surface deep-seated issues.

Most companies use organization-wide surveys to channel their employees' many voices into clear themes, in hopes that these themes will point toward useful action. These surveys are appreciated and important. At a minimum, they are a signal to employees that their opinions matter and that they have mechanisms through which their perspectives can be heard.

Too often, however, the results of these surveys fail to illuminate what's really going on in an organization. There are a few reasons for this:

- People are skeptical about the anonymity of their answers. It's hard for employees to believe that anything they write or say through a company interface—even via a survey that promises confidentiality—is truly anonymous.

- Positivity bias is a powerful, well-documented force. People have a natural inclination to answer questions in the affirmative.

- Most surveys are too broad. When leaders survey their organization, they often strive for comprehensiveness.

When it comes to culture and people, remember that "not everything that counts can be counted and not everything that can be counted, counts."

As rewarding as it will be to try to find hard metrics for culture early on, you may have to accept that some parts of culture cannot be measured—sometimes you instead have to rely on what you see, hear, and feel. As CEO, you need to get comfortable reading, acting, and reporting on such intangible measures. Consider exploring these factors:

- **What stories are being told?** This will tell you much about what is praised and what is demonized.

- **What behaviors were the former CEO and leadership team role modeling?** Is this what people are aspiring to be or the reason people are leaving?

- **How confident are you that people are acting in the right way?** What formal and informal aspects are promoting or inhibiting the right behaviors?

- **What processes and systems govern the organization?** What are people rewarded and praised for—and what is ignored?

- **Are there any trouble spots in the organization?** Are you aware of poor behavior? Does the organization lack diversity? Is there accountability? Are ethical standards unclear?

Legacy Culture

Some CEOs have the view that their organizational culture is good or bad based purely on the players, values, and behaviors that exist today. They believe that if they can just remove the bad actors and address the bad behaviors, the culture will improve.

While this can be true, it's important to remember that bad actors can cast a long shadow, and continue to influence values and behaviors long after they have left the organization. There is a story about an experiment that clearly explains this phenomenon (note that there is debate about whether this experiment ever happened, but I will use it as an example either way).

It involved five chimpanzees in an area together. A bunch of bananas were placed up high. When one of the

(continued)

monkeys tried to access the bananas, all the monkeys were sprayed with cold water. When a second monkey also tried to access the bananas, all the monkeys were sprayed once more. After a couple of attempts, the monkeys started to self-regulate each other, acting violently toward any monkey that attempted to get the bananas.

Over a period of time, the researchers swapped out the monkeys one by one. Each time a new monkey was introduced, and tried to get the bananas, the other monkeys attacked it. This behavior continued when all the monkeys were new, that is, none had ever been sprayed with cold water.

The example highlights how norms, behaviors, and culture can live on well after the shaping event or the individual driving the behavior has gone.

Removing the bad actors from your organization is important and you should do it as soon as you can. However, that might not be enough to remove the behavior or beliefs. People train others; they onboard them in the ways of the business as they were shown. Good and bad behavior is passed along. You need to help people question why they are doing things.

Everybody Wants Change; No One Wants to Change

Five frogs are sitting on a log and four decide to jump off. How many frogs are left?*

When you start your role as the new CEO, there will be an expectation that you will make things better, that you will fix the things that are wrong, and improve the things that are good—that you will change things.

As you move around the organization, you will have conversations about what needs fixing. People will talk favorably about change and the benefits that it will bring. You will feel encouraged about pushing it through: "People are asking for it; they desperately want it." It will play nicely to the feeling that you can make a positive, if not enormous, difference here.

Remember, people will agree with you more now that you are CEO; they will avoid challenging you or upsetting you. You will hear "yes" to a lot of things that you want to hear "yes" to.

As you talk about the future vision and potential greatness, people will see your passion and will nod and agree. You will want to hear that they're up for it as that will likely have been one of your concerns coming into the role. Positive reinforcement makes you feel great: "They also see the need for change and are behind it." Some, yes, but unlikely all.

Don't mistake the understanding for the *need* to change with the *willingness* to change. The adage is true: Everyone wants change; no one wants to change.

A better way to interpret people's enthusiasm for change is to hear: "Yes, we absolutely need change; go and make those changes—over there. Just don't change the things I am working on."

Remember that change is difficult and that there is considerable ground to cover between agreeing that change is necessary and actually making the change. And even more ground to cover before the change is embedded.

People Doing Things Right versus Doing the Right Things

Of course, you want an organization where people do the things they need to do in the *right way*. That is obvious. If they aren't doing this, the potential for negative consequences (for your organization and you personally) is vast—no CEO wants to be in front of a committee hearing or government inquiry.

It's natural to reward and promote people who do things in the *right way*. It is not a negative thing or a bad way to operate. In fact, for many of the roles in organizations, it is crucial—check the plane engine, check the bank transfers, follow the checklist before operating. No debate.

But what if the thing they are doing in the *right way* is actually the *wrong* thing to do? Examples might include a compensation model that rewards employees to sell or package the offering in a way that is less beneficial for the client, or a process that rewards people avoiding certain reporting that would benefit the data collection internally.

Many examples exist of businesses having processes, procedures, or rules that were suitable at one time, but that now make it hard for people to do the right thing. In these cases, a frontline employee will often design and implement a workaround—either with or without management approval—because it is the *"right thing to do."*

(It is even worse when the process or issue is one that management understands is wrong, but they keep it in place because it benefits them or their division financially.)

So, remember there can be a difference between doing things in the *right way* and *doing the right things*. When you are new in a role and you are learning and assessing both the people and the culture, try to look for this distinction.

(This is particularly the case if you're an external hire, but even internal hires should be on the lookout and keep asking themselves if they're being objective enough.)

Ultimately, you want people to be doing things the *right way,* but make sure they are also aware of and making the choices to *do the right things.* Sometimes doing the *right thing* is not what's obvious or not what's being praised and rewarded.

Shifting the Culture

I will assume that you have come across the variations of the saying, "Culture eats strategy for breakfast/lunch/fun, etc." You should also have an understanding that cultures are difficult to change, and yet, if you are like so many CEOs in transition, change it you must; otherwise, you will not be able to deliver the outcomes you have promised.

Missionaries, Not Mercenaries

By Margot McShane, Managing Director at RRA

When Doug Mack, the former CEO of Fanatics, looked to refresh the company culture he set out on a roadshow, called *Mission, Vision, Culture,* visiting every office and meeting with every employee to crystalize his understanding of where Fanatics was and where it needed to be.

From the hundreds of conversations he had, Doug sat down and penned a new, ambitious mission for Fanatics: to become a $5-billion global company and the No. 1 fan brand in the world.

(continued)

Doug also set out the company's five core values that would serve as a guiding light: This was a company built by fans, for fans; Working as "One Fanatics," winning as a team; Valuing execution and agility over talk; Delivering innovative products and fan experiences (where others may try to be the low cost provider); and that they were missionaries, not mercenaries.

"I stole that last one from John Doerr—and I was honest about that," Doug joked. "John talked about being missionaries, not mercenaries when I was at One Kings Lane. I loved it. And I really felt that we needed to be clear that, at Fanatics, people are here for the love of the game, not because they think it's a hot internet company."

The articulation of the company's mission and values "really lit people up," Doug said. He himself kept coming back to it as he made decisions about whom to hire, who fitted in on the team, whom to advance, whom to reward, and what they celebrated when they were together. (To this end, at Town Halls, Doug made a point of highlighting stories of people—from the junior ranks to the top team—who'd gone out of their way to make a fan experience better).

"The roadshow was the most important week in the history of the company. I remember saying, 'Hey, we're never going to be better than Nike in sports marketing, and we're never going to out-compete Amazon's enormous scale. So, we've got to win on something, and it's got to be on being united, fan-focused, and moving really fast.'"

Doug continued, "It's really worked. I mean, we've out-executed Amazon so far, and Nike is one of our biggest and most important partners. I can't emphasize enough how fixing the culture was the jet fuel for getting us to where we are today."

If this is your first time in the CEO role, what you might experience is the difference between being part of a culture and being ultimately responsible for a culture. As a senior executive, you have probably worked in several organizational cultures throughout your career. In your senior roles, you would also have had a role as a key culture carrier, a member of the executive team whose actions and behaviors either did or did not represent the desired values of the organization.

However, now, as CEO, you are the masthead for your organizational culture. When we ask CEOs to name the things that only they can do, the most common answer is to represent and drive the culture. They see it as their ultimate responsibility that they shape and form the culture and the acceptable behaviors. They often acknowledge the role the executive team and the senior management team play, but they ultimately recognize that it is their behavior as CEO that the organization looks at when determining what the culture is here.

When I asked how long it took new CEOs to move the culture from where it was when they took on the role to where they wanted it to be, the average response was 12 months. Changing your culture takes time. It is something that you start on immediately just by how you show up, what you say, and what you do (and don't do).[4]

Throughout the book, we met Mark Clouse, who inherited a significant turnaround situation when he became Campbell's CEO in 2019. That year, the company celebrated its 150th anniversary, but for some time had been struggling to respond to rapidly changing market dynamics, drive relevancy, and maximize shareholder value. In the year before Mark took the helm, Campbell's gross profits were down 3.7%.

But Mark told me that he didn't just face a profound business turnaround. He would also need to push ahead with a "material cultural transformation"—something that he appears to have pulled off, having helped Campbell's exceed its own financial expectations for four consecutive quarters in his first year. The following year, gross profits were up 11%.[5]

His first task had been to embed a performance-driven culture across the company. "When I joined only about 50% of the company had stated objectives," he told me. "In a world where you're trying to drive accountability and create alignment to a new strategy or direction, having a mechanism for setting goals and then tracking progress against them on an individual basis was a big priority for me."

Mark and his team went about setting a clear strategy so that everyone understood the direction the company was heading, and how their work and objectives connected to it. This four-pillar strategy enabled the creation of a simple but effective goal-setting scorecard for all employees that's still used today.

Once that was established, Mark went to work on what he referred to as the "hearts and minds" of the company's 14,000-plus employees. It entailed a four-step process that begins with "brokering hope." "It might sound a bit dramatic, but the first order of business is always to create hope. It's a very effective way of thinking about what you're trying to do."

But Mark is clear that fostering hope wasn't just about building a castle in the sky. "If you walk in on Day One to a business that was at a stage where Campbell's was and start talking immediately about how next quarter we're going to be the best food company in America, you lose all credibility," he said.

He added, "My job was to remind people how great these brands were. And that if we could breathe life into them, we had a real opportunity to demonstrate that these businesses are still relevant."

Next, Mark moves onto fostering belief.

"I was constantly looking in those early days for quick wins. And usually, the good news is if you're coming into a business that's been losing, the bar is actually quite low. So, your ability to find things that you can improve upon quickly can be quite helpful because that will begin to transition people from hope to belief: 'Oh wow, we grew soup this quarter, we grew our market share. Yes, we can win.'"

After belief, comes confidence. "Now, people start showing up, expecting our businesses to succeed and to win. The ultimate goal is ownership. Now, I'm not sure you ever truly arrive there, but ownership is the ultimate destination. People not only expect to win, but they will not accept losing. They develop a mindset where they will not allow the company to *not* win.

Mark's framework—from hope to ownership—was one established at West Point and the Army, then honed over a 30-year corporate career. "My time at Pinnacle helped me because no one believed those brands could grow, and we made it the fastest-growing food company for two years in a row. So, when people at Campbell's have doubted our ability to grow, I always joke, 'Look, you think growing soup is hard? Try growing pickles.'"

The New CEO Checklist

- **Get out the corner office.** The benefits of walking the halls flow in two directions. It gives you a chance to "set the tone" of the culture you want and to "hear the echo" from the frontline about the way things really work across the organization.

- **Look beyond the culture survey.** No single metric can paint a full picture of your organization's culture. While culture surveys are important, find other ways to get answers to the tough questions about how people think, feel, act, and behave.

- **Be the change you want to see.** Your actions— and those of your leadership team—are the cultural beacon for the rest of the organization. Actions speak louder than words. Are you walking the talk, or just talking the talk?

- **Fold the seatbelts.** Changing culture is hard—and despite what you may hear otherwise, people are inherently resistant to change. Get out to the frontline and engage. As Jetstar's Stephanie Tully said, "Culture is changed one conversation at a time."

- **Foster hope.** To bring the entire organization along on your culture journey, you first need to set the vision of where you are headed. Remind everyone of the reason the organization (and you) are here—and the opportunities that lay ahead if you double down on your strengths.

---

*The logical answer to the question about the frogs is that one frog is left on the log. However, the likely answer is five. Why? Because there is a big difference between deciding to do something and actually doing it.

PART IV

Less of a Marathon, More a Series of Sprints

CHAPTER 11

If I Could Do It All Over Again

A saying that I love is, "Experience is what you get just after you needed it." This will, in part, be the case for your transition. I say "in part" because here you do have the ability to learn from others who have gone before you and held the role that only a very small percentage of the world's population ever holds— being the new CEO.

If you had an opportunity to sit with all the CEOs I have featured, interviewed, surveyed, and supported in this book, and could ask them one question, what would it be?

My guess is that you would probably ask, "What is the one piece of advice you would give me, as a new CEO, to be successful in my transition?" Another one might be, "If you had your transition again, would you do anything differently?"

So, here I share a collection of invaluable advice and hindsight from some of your peers, from those who have done it, and done it well.

Ramon Laguarta, CEO, PepsiCo

"As a new CEO, you need to be aware that your first six months are so important in terms of your success. If you get it right, you build momentum, which will help carry through the changes and initiatives that you need to deliver during the rest of your tenure.

"The other thing is that, in terms of cultural change, you can't underestimate the power of being a new leader in a room. From the start, I encouraged people to come to meetings empowered to share their views and opinions, which sent a clear signal that this was going to be the new way. Out of those early conversations, we came up with the behaviors that we wanted to foster. Today, you can go to any factory, warehouse, sales office, or anywhere else in the company and they are being lived.

"Lastly, be very conscious you don't have all the information. Unless you listen, with intention and real focus, people will tell you what you want to hear. That is a big risk, a huge risk."

Mark Clouse, CEO, Campbell's

"If I could go back, there would be a couple of places where I would have prioritized stability over progress. And other areas that I would have tried to be more aggressive and bite off a bit more. Finding that balance is tough. If I could do it again, I would have moved faster. Every CEO will likely have similar thoughts with the benefit of hindsight.

"My other piece of advice is to make your priorities and your communication clear. Keep it simple. Be structured and let that set your agenda. Don't try to fix every leaky pipe. If you do, odds are that you're not going to get the traction that you need. Do what is necessary to move the company forward and get clear about the sequencing. Work out where you are, where you need to go, and what needs to be true in order to get there. What needs to be true is often speed. Let that set your priority in a turnaround situation. Even if you are only 70% right, you're still making progress—and that is so important for organizations that have been losing."

Marc Bitzer, CEO, Whirlpool

"Never forget that you are here to serve. Serve the organization first, then your team, and then long afterward yourself. Too many CEOs confuse that sequence and overstay their time in the job. They think it's about them. But nobody is bigger than an organization.

"You need to be confident, but you still need to stay humble. People read so much into your everyday behaviors. CEOs are associated with being arrogant. So, yes, you have to be confident, but you better stay humble.

"Remember the massive impact you have on the people in your organization. The things you turn up to and things you don't send a big signal. If I change my calendar, a hundred people across the organization now feel they have to change their own meetings to accommodate me. You think you're being flexible, but in reality, you just add to the chaos. Lastly, never get used to the power and never let yourself be defined by your title. It will drive you crazy. I still say to myself regularly, 'I'm a hired manager. It feels like my company, but ultimately, I am a salaried employee.'"

Stephanie Tully, CEO, Jetstar

"Listen. Really listen. Exhaust yourself listening. Be seen as someone who is committed to hearing what people really think and feel across the organization.

"Also listen to those who tell you that it is a lonely role. You will need to find your own drive and new connections internally and externally. One thing that has been invaluable to me is finding the counsel of someone who has been involved in other CEO successions and transitions to bounce stuff off. Having someone external who you can ask really silly questions to and in return get some ideas about how to structure your thoughts and planning was so helpful to me early on."

Sanjiv Lamba, CEO, Linde plc

"Three things: First, the culture of the organization matters. I know every management author says it. But for a new CEO coming in, the culture of the organization and how well you understand it is so critical for success. The saying is true: Culture *will* eat strategy for breakfast, lunch, dinner, and dessert. Do not underestimate it. And if you can, leverage it.

"Second, know your business inside out. It doesn't matter whether you're coming from the outside or coming from within. Be curious. Ask the questions you need to ask. There is no such thing as a bad question.

"And third, make sure that you understand your board and engage them early and often. Don't underestimate that you need to make the effort. It's critical to your success."

Hans Vestberg, CEO, Verizon

"Prepare well for your role. Before becoming CEO, write down what you know and what you want or need to do. If you go in blind and go with the flow, you will get lost and pulled in many directions. There will be so many brilliant people around you—one week you'll find a great person who said one thing, then weeks later you'll talk to yet another brilliant person with a different perspective. If you don't have a plan, you run the risk of chopping and changing your ideas and getting blown off course.

"I've seen firsthand how very senior executives come in without a clear idea of what they are going to do. As a result, they make decisions that are not grounded, and that are either wrong or not right enough. There's no way you will succeed without some sort of plan or map, which you adjust as you go. You need to make a map for yourself, which you can then course-correct as you get better information. Whatever you do, don't go in blind.

"To help my senior leaders avoid this, I ask them to do a 'Boss Contract' before they start where they outline what they are committed to doing, what behavioral aspects they will bring, and how they will measure their success. This process drives extreme clarity for both of us, plus increases their confidence that they are working to deliver the right outcomes. Being clear on what is expected of your leaders is a critical responsibility as CEO."

Carol Tomé, CEO, UPS

"Respect the past but be different. Find that balance; it's important to your success.

"Understand that, in your role as CEO, you are at the intersection of all contradictions, like short-term versus long-term, and values versus productivity. It's a hard place to be.

"You rarely get a clean shot at things. More often, you face a paradox, or a series of decisions and judgment calls where you are picking the 'least-worse option.' You must think through that really carefully. Make sure you have the right people on your team who will help you do this.

"Lastly, don't let your values take you down a path that you're not going to be happy with."

Doug Mack, Former CEO, Fanatics

"Disproportionately in the early days, focus on your leaders. You will struggle to carry the whole thing by yourself— and you are only going to get as far as the star talent on your team. It's very unlikely you came in as a new CEO because there was a great team. Odds are, this will not be the case.

"A potential mistake is to remain fixed on the way things were done at your previous organization. There are two issues with this. First, it can constrain your thinking if you believe the formula where you came from was fully optimized and will work here. You have a new piece of clay to mold, and you need to work out what makes sense in your new company and what doesn't. The second, frankly, is that it can be super annoying for your team.

"Be really thoughtful about bringing context and patterns from the past. Learn the business you are joining, apply what's relevant, and filter out what's not. This also applies to your hiring decisions. Don't just hire the best people you already know. Hire the best people in the world.

"Lastly, my view is that your culture can never be good enough. So, even if you've inherited a good culture, figure out how to make it a great one."

Paula MacKenzie, CEO, PizzaExpress

"First, get a support structure in place early. Work out who is on your brain train and who ultimately has your back. This won't necessarily be the chair or the board. Everybody in the organization reports to you, so that's not that useful either. Find your trusted sounding board.

"Second, people think you will start telling them what to do from the moment you walk in the door. Early on, you need to decide how to communicate what you are doing. When you are the new CEO, people want to know what you are thinking, what you are doing, what you are learning, and how you are learning it. Sharing this opens up great lines of early feedback.

"Something I found helpful was writing a weekly newsletter to the organization. I committed to writing it for 10 weeks. It really was a labor of love—the last thing you want to do when you are exhausted at the end of the week. But it went down brilliantly. People felt like they knew me. So, I still do it."

Ron Williams, Former Chairman & CEO of Aetna, CEO of RW2 Enterprises

"First, think early and often about your end goal. Your job is to run the organization effectively on your watch, but more importantly, to leave it well positioned for the next CEO. Second, recognize that the CEO role is distinctly different to what you have been doing before. The third piece of advice would be reach out and learn from others who have been where you are going.

"I would add that it is also important to understand that all of your actions are magnified, so your behavior, communication, and engagement has to be highly consistent. People want to know who is showing up today. If you're mercurial one day and calm the next, people will be confused. You have to be your authentic self, obviously. But you need to figure out what that means and operate in that range.

"Lastly, never let anything pass in front of you that you do not understand. If you do, it will come back to haunt you. Just say that you don't understand."

Alan Beacham, CEO, Toll Group

"Your context is really important. If you're internal, you need to get clear on your narrative. If you're external, you need to work out how to access the organization effectively to understand it to the level that you need.

"Set time frames for your early actions and plan the sequencing of things that you have decided absolutely need to happen, such as when you address the culture, your strategy, or your top team assessment. You need a plan that sets you up for success.

"The other piece of advice would be that speed is your friend, but not at all costs. If you come in with a huge agenda for change, and make big moves really early, you'll find that the organization fails to implement and execute it. Don't go so fast that you break the business."

Winnie Park, CEO, Forever 21

"You're not part of a team anymore. You don't belong to a functional group. It's the first time in your life where you don't have that. You need to forge a sense of 'we're all in this together' with your SLT. You will need it almost as much as they will—and it's something you have to consciously cultivate. It doesn't just happen. Never take that for granted.

"The advice I was given was that when you're a CEO you will feel self-conscious of your performance all the time because you could be let go at any time. But at some point, you're going to have to take a step back and say to yourself, 'They need me as much as I need them.' It will give you the courage to make the right decisions. I thought that was great advice.

"I will also say that it's important to prioritize progress over perfection. We're often rewarded in the roles before we become a CEO for being perfect—for consistently hitting it out of the park, for projecting the right image, or being able to articulate your view to a board or a group of employees. You are *rewarded* for your perfectionism. But aiming for perfectionism as a CEO will only slow you down. Being a CEO is the most humbling position. You will make a lot of mistakes. So, you've got to forgive yourself and somehow embrace progress and not perfection. That's hard."

André Lacroix, CEO, Intertek

Think of your transition as a springboard—something that will take you to the next level. If you don't, you won't make the most of this opportunity in front of you. Before you start, your stakeholders give you the rare luxury of time to think about what you want to achieve and to get ready. You need to take it. Your transition is a very important part of your journey. And if you get it wrong, you're not going to succeed. So, take the time to be super sharp. Invest a lot of time in your preparation because the quality of your thinking will be linked to the amount of time you invest. Getting ready is extremely, extremely important.

Lyssa McGowan, CEO, Pets at Home

"Understand that being a CEO is a different job. The learning curve is steep and a lot of what got you into this role isn't what will make you successful in this role. In the past, when things got tough, I succeeded by speeding up and getting things done. As a CEO, when things get tough, I actually need to slow down and create space to bring people towards a solution.

"You need confidence and courage in your convictions. But you should always have one small part of your brain asking, 'What if I'm wrong?' Hubris can be a dangerous thing.

"Finally, as Maya Angelou said, 'People won't remember what you said or what you did, but they will never forget how you made them feel.' I'll probably see most of our 16,000 colleagues maybe once or twice in our careers. For me, that's 15 minutes of my day. So, if I walk into a store and say, 'Why is that on the floor?' that's the impression they take away pretty much forever. Whereas sitting down with them at the back of the store, having a cup of tea, or chatting to customers leaves a very different impression. Always be cognizant of that: even if you are having a bad day or it's the eighth store visit of the day, your people will never forget how you made them feel."

Final Thoughts

In the famous scene from *Jaws*, when the unlikely band of shark hunters first get a good look at the monster, Chief Brody says the famous line, "We're gonna need a bigger boat!" What had seemed a suitably sized craft when they left the wharf, was now clearly too small. The equipment they thought would be enough to cope, would not be.

The parallel for your transition is that you may, like many new CEOs, approach the role thinking that you can easily cope. After all, you've already juggled the demands of being a successful senior executive. You might be thinking, "I've got this, this is what I do well."

For many, it can be a shock to find out they need a bigger boat.

The truth is that your transition to becoming the new CEO—for the first, second, or third time—will be one of the hardest challenges of your career. It will test you to your limit.

It is often helpful to remember that, while you belong to an exclusive club, many people have held the role before you. And many more will hold it again, long after you have stepped down. While some will inevitably fail to deliver, many more will have survived, and more importantly, thrived as CEO.

The key is to go in with your eyes open. It's about admitting you don't have all the answers and opening yourself up to learning—from those who have gone before and from those rooting for your success.

As I said in the Introduction, I have one of the best jobs. It is a great and rare privilege to be a trusted advisor alongside so many phenomenal leaders as they go through this uniquely challenging period of being the new CEO.

My thoughts, ideas, observations, and advice are woven throughout this book. But now I get the opportunity to leave you with some final thoughts to bring it all together, to help ground you, and to help you navigate the inevitable psychological rollercoaster that being the new CEO can be.

Being CEO is a privilege, not a right. Yes, you have earned it and you deserve it, but that does not diminish the fact that it is a great honor to be chosen. Make sure that you display real gratitude for the opportunity to occupy the role. This does not weaken your leadership, it does the opposite. People make the choice to follow you every day they decide to stay in your organization. They can opt out at any point. Remember this and express a healthy gratitude for the opportunity to serve as their leader, early and often.

Be humble. You will not be ready. No one ever is. Even those who have been groomed and developed as the CEO successor find the complexity and demands of the role more than they expected. As prepared as you feel you are, you are unlikely to be ready for the challenges that face you as CEO. This is normal. It is not a negative reflection on your capability nor your potential to be a great CEO. It is simply a factor that there is no CEO sandbox. Get support, from as many sources as you need.

It's the role, not you. You should be proud to be CEO. It is a great honor and responsibility. But remember your role is also an office—the office of the CEO. Others have occupied it and others will hold it after you. Think about this when the invitations start to pour in for conferences, events, board roles, and speaking engagements. You have a lot to do and many stakeholders to work with, so be careful to not get distracted by your newfound popularity. As one new CEO who had been invited to a major suppliers' annual ski trip, told me, "How could I espouse working harder with a goggle tan?"

The position is not your identity. High egos and CEOs have gone together in stories and real life for decades. In fact, when there is a successful CEO who is low-ego, it is lauded as unique and rare. As CEO, you are important and you will feel important most places you go, but remember your position is not your identity. It is easy to forget this. This is a role that you have probably coveted for many years and worked tirelessly to achieve. Keep people around you who can help you stay grounded—and to help you remember which balls are made of glass.

As you go through the CEO transition, you will be focusing deeply on yourself—your actions, your observations, your feelings. This is normal—for all the reasons outlined in this book. But consider this valuable perspective from Sanjiv Lamba, CEO of Linde plc, who is clear about the importance of widening your aperture. "We talk about the CEO transition as something that only a CEO goes through, but it's complete nonsense," he told me.

"That is a somewhat self-centered, CEO perspective. Yes, a CEO transition is very stressful, maybe even traumatic for you. But you also need to remember that it is equally stressful for the organization, too. It should actually be called an organizational transition, not a CEO transition."

Sanjiv added, "The reality is that the organization can potentially come to a standstill asking, 'What should we expect? What is going to happen? Is everything going to change?' There is a huge amount of stress, and it's up to you as the new CEO to solve that."

* * *

The greatest variable in the transition is, of course, you. How you manage yourself during this time will make the difference. How you come to terms with the loneliness. How you keep your biases from negatively affecting your progress and others around you. How you manage your internal pressure around action. How you manage your poker face and communication. How you balance your time and energy, manage your outside commitments and exercise, and show up authentically. How you build relationships. How you act as the new CEO.

The quicker you can ground and anchor yourself, the quicker you will anchor and ground your organization—and the quicker you will deliver success (both for your business, and for yourself).

Good luck! We are all cheering for your success.

Ty

Endnotes

Introduction

1. Global CEO Turnover Index. (2022). Russell Reynolds Associates. https://www.russellreynolds.com/en/insights/reports-surveys/global-ceo-turnover-index
2. Kerr, Peter, and Thompson, Brad. (2023 August 28). Fortescue mining boss Fiona Hick walks. *AFR Magazine*. https://www.afr.com/companies/mining/fortescue-mining-boss-fiona-hick-walks-20230828-p5dzuo

Chapter 1

1. Saporito, Thomas J. (2012 February 15). It's time to acknowledge CEO loneliness. *Harvard Business Review*. https://hbr.org/2012/02/its-time-to-acknowledge-ceo-lo
2. Varley, Len. (2023 January 2). Jetstar—The year 2022 in review. *Aviation Source News*. https://aviationsourcenews.com/analysis/jetstar-the-year-2022-in-review/
3. Wiggins, Ty, and Davies, Rebecca. (2024). CEO transitions: Defining Success in the First 12 Months. Russell Reynolds Associates.

Chapter 2

1. Wiggins, Ty. (2019). An investigation of factors that promote and inhibit performance during leadership transitions, Sydney Business School, University of Wollongong. https://ro.uow.edu.au/theses1/541/

Chapter 3

1. Blanding, Michael. (2021 May 12). The hard truth about being a CEO. Harvard Business School Working Knowledge. https://hbswk.hbs.edu/item/the-hard-truth-about-being-a-ceo
2. Gregersen, Hal. (2017 March–April). Bursting the CEO bubble. *Harvard Business Review*. https://hbr.org/2017/03/bursting-the-ceo-bubble
3. Stamoulis, Dean, Handcock, Tom, and Safferstone, Todd. (2022 September 2). Stretched too thin? Are CEOs happy with how they spend their time? Russell Reynolds Associates. https://www.russellreynolds.com/en/insights/articles/stretched-too-thin-are-ceos-happy-with-how-they-spend-their-time
4. Lucas, Amelia. (2023 March 23). Starbucks CEO says he'll work a shift at the company's cafes once a month. CNBC. https://www.cnbc.com/2023/03/23/new-starbucks-ceo-says-hell-work-a-shift-at-its-cafes-once-a-month.html
5. Bove, Tristan. (2023 April 8). Uber's CEO moonlighted as a driver and it changed the way he operates the company. *Fortune*. https://fortune.com/2023/04/07/uber-ceo-moonlights-as-driver/
6. Saul, Derek. (2022 January 19). Billionaire Airbnb CEO Brian Chesky will live full-time in Airbnb properties. *Forbes*. https://www.forbes.com/SITES/DEREKSAUL/2022/01/18/BILLIONAIRE-AIRBNB-CEO-BRIAN-CHESKY-WILL-LIVE-FULL-TIME-IN-AIRBNB-PROPERTIES/?sh=2b8a97793e5d

Chapter 4

1. Birshan, Michael, Meakin, Tom, and Strovink, Kurt. (2016 May 20). How new CEOs can boost their odds of success. McKinsey. https://www.mckinsey.com/featured-insights/leadership/how-new-ceos-can-boost-their-odds-of-success

Chapter 5

1. Pringle, Eleanor. (2023 March 29). Microsoft CEO Satya Nadella's top piece of career advice. *Fortune*. https://fortune .com/2023/03/29/microsoft-ceo-satya-nadella-best-career-advice
2. Satya Nadella email to employees on first day as CEO (2014 February 4). *Microsoft News Center*. https://news.microsoft .com/2014/02/04/satya-nadella-email-to-employees-on-first-day-as-ceo/
3. Pringle, Eleanor. (2023 March 29). Microsoft CEO Satya Nadella's top piece of career advice. *Fortune*. https://fortune .com/2023/03/29/microsoft-ceo-satya-nadella-best-career-advice/
4. Covey, Stephen M.R. (2006). *The speed of trust: The one thing that changes everything*. Simon & Schuster.
5. Swant, Marty. (2021 April 19). Silence is not an option: Research shows consumers expect CEOs to take a stand on political issues. *Forbes*. https://www.forbes.com/sites/ martyswant/2021/04/19/silence-is-not-an-option-research-shows-consumers-expect-ceos-to-take-a-stand-on-political-issues
6. Valadon, Olga. (2023 October 17). What we get wrong about empathic leadership. *Harvard Business Review*. https://hbr .org/2023/10/what-we-get-wrong-about-empathic-leadership

Chapter 6

1. Stamoulis, Dean, Handcock, Tom, and Safferstone, Todd. (2022 September 2). Stretched too thin? Are CEOs happy with how they spend their time? Russell Reynolds Associates. https://www.russellreynolds.com/en/insights/articles/ stretched-too-thin-are-ceos-happy-with-how-they-spend-their-time

2. "Five balls of life" quote misattributed to Sundar Pichai. (2021 November 24). *Reuters Fact Check*. Reuters.com. https://www.reuters.com/article/factcheck-quote-sundar-pichai-idUSL1N2SE1SE/

3. Wiggins, Ty, and Davies, Rebecca. (2024). CEO transitions: Defining Success in the First 12 Months. Russell Reynolds Associates.

4. Stamoulis, Dean, Handcock, Tom, and Safferstone, Todd. (2022 September 2). Stretched too thin? Are CEOs happy with how they spend their time? Russell Reynolds Associates. https://www.russellreynolds.com/en/insights/articles/stretched-too-thin-are-ceos-happy-with-how-they-spend-their-time

5. Leadership for the decade of action. (2020). Russell Reynolds Associates and the United Nations Global Compact. https://www.russellreynolds.com/en/leadership-decade-action

6. Trust your gut: AXA's Thomas Buberl talks transformation and reinvention. (2022 May 25). *Redefiners Podcast Series*, Russell Reynolds Associates. https://www.russellreynolds.com/en/insights/podcasts/trust-your-gut-axas-thomas-buberl-talks-transformation-and-reinvention

Chapter 7

1. Business overall has been very good, says Fanatics CEO Michael Rubin (2023 February 13). *Closing Bell*. CNBC.com https://www.cnbc.com/video/2023/02/13/business-overall-has-been-very-good-says-fanatics-ceo-michael-rubin.html.

2. Wiggins, Ty, and Davies, Rebecca. (2024). CEO transitions: Defining Success in the First 12 Months. Russell Reynolds Associates.

3. Wiggins, Ty, and Davies, Rebecca. (2024). CEO transitions: Defining Success in the First 12 Months. Russell Reynolds Associates.
4. Wiggins, Ty, and Davies, Rebecca. (2024). CEO transitions: Defining Success in the First 12 Months. Russell Reynolds Associates.

Chapter 8

1. Tomé, Carol B. (2021 September–October).The CEO of UPS on taking the reins amid surging pandemic demand. *Harvard Business Review*. https://hbr.org/2021/09/the-ceo-of-ups-on-taking-the-reins-amid-surging-pandemic-demand
2. Tomé, Carol B. (2021 September–October). The CEO of UPS on taking the reins amid surging pandemic demand. *Harvard Business Review*. https://hbr.org/2021/09/the-ceo-of-ups-on-taking-the-reins-amid-surging-pandemic-demand
3. Krueger, Dana, and Hinds, Jim. (2022 September 1). C-suite performance: Are you thinking about your top team in the right way? Russell Reynolds Associates. https://www.russellreynolds.com/en/insights/articles/c-suite-performance-are-you-thinking-about-your-top-team-in-the-right-way
4. Abramowicz, Ilana, Ligthart, Pieter, Hinds, Jim, and Lange, David. (2021 January 29). Igniting high performance: How Top Teams Navigate Four Essential Tensions. Russell Reynolds Associates. https://www.russellreynolds.com/en/insights/articles/c-suite-performance-are-you-thinking-about-your-top-team-in-the-right-way
5. Dixon-Fyle, Sundiatu, Dolan, Kevin, Hunt, Dame Vivian, and Price, Sara. (2020 May 19). Diversity wins: How inclusion matters. McKinsey. https://www.mckinsey.com/featured-insights/diversity-and-inclusion/diversity-wins-how-inclusion-matters

6. Leading with vulnerability with bestselling author Jacob Morgan. (2023 November 1). Season 3, Episode 16. *Redefiners Podcast Series*, Russell Reynolds Associates. https://www.russellreynolds.com/en/insights/podcasts/leading-with-vulnerability-with-bestselling-author-jacob-morgan

Chapter 9

1. Wiggins, Ty, and Davies, Rebecca. (2024). CEO transitions: Defining Success in the First 12 Months. Russell Reynolds Associates.
2. Wiggins, Ty, and Davies, Rebecca. (2024). CEO transitions: Defining Success in the First 12 Months. Russell Reynolds Associates.

Chapter 10

1. The future of Australia's aviation sector in the context of COVID-19 and conditions post pandemic. (2022 March). Parliament of Australia. https://www.aph.gov.au/parliamentary_business/committees/senate/rural_and_regional_affairs_and_transport/covidaviation/report/
2. Anderson, Gretchen, Christiansen, Leah, Dineen, Sean, et al. (2022 December 12). Why bad things happen to good companies: A risk culture study. Russell Reynolds Associates. https://www.russellreynolds.com/en/insights/articles/why-bad-things-happen-to-good-companies
3. Anderson, Gretchen, Christianson, Leah, Wimpfheimer, Eric, and Wood, Andrew. (2022 August 31). Measurement mindset: A practical approach for understanding culture. Russell Reynolds Associates. https://www.russellreynolds.com/en/insights/articles/measurement-mindset-a-practical-approach-for-understanding-culture

4. Wiggins, Ty, and Davies, Rebecca. (2024). CEO transitions: Defining Success in the First 12 Months. Russell Reynolds Associates.

5. Campbell's 2018 Annual Report and Campbell's 2021 Annual Report. https://investor.campbellsoupcompany.com/financials/annual-reports/default.aspx

Acknowledgments

While this was an idea borne from the work I am so privileged to be able to do, it would not have happened without the support of so many.

Thank you to all the CEOs who agreed to share their experiences in this book—named and unnamed. By being so generous with your time and experiences, you have invested in the next generation of CEOs.

Thank you to the 50+ CEO clients who trusted me to support them through such a challenging time and allowed me to be part of their journey. I am sure I gained more than I gave.

Thank you to Amy Scissons for having the foresight and guts to push RRA to start sharing our rich experiences in books—and the RRA Marketing team who believed in, supported, and promoted this one from the start.

Thank you to our CEO Constantine Alexandrakis for your support. I appreciate the faith and the investment.

Thank you to Clarke Murphy and Jenna Fisher for paving the way for me to reap all the benefits of your hard work.

To my partners on the book—Justus O'Brien, Laura Sanderson, Margot McShane, Rusty O'Kelley, and Steve Langton—thank you for bringing your fantastic clients to this project, adding your valuable insights to the interviews, for your ongoing support, and for having the confidence in my ability to write this book.

Susie Sell, thank you for helping me to better articulate my thoughts and ideas, and pushing me to write a much better book. And (see what I did there) for being the only person other than Chief Martin Brody to kill Jaws—and then somehow bring it back from the dead.

Thank you to Rebecca Davies, for your support on the qualitative research interviews during the last year or more, and for being the producer of the best box and whisker graphs this side of Barcelona.

To the other colleagues who supported this book: David Lange, Sean Dineen, Maja Hadziomerovic, Norm Yustin, Luke Meynell, Eric Wimpfheimer, Marie-Osmonde Le Roy de Lanauze-Molines, Ben Jones, Tom Handcock, and all the ones I missed—thank you.

Thank you also to Dr. Gordon Spence and Dr. Ananda Wickramasinghe for playing the critical (and often frustrating) role of supervisors through my Ph.D. Also, to Dr. Grace McCarthy for the often gentle yet frank push to try harder.

Thank you to Wayne and Donna Condon for many years of business partnership, friendship, support, and belief that I could do well and always do more.

Finally, to my partner, parents, family, and friends who both prop me up and keep me grounded, never letting me get too overwhelmed, nor too full of myself. They say you are a reflection of those who love you, and my reflection is beautiful—thank you all so very, very much.

Ty

About the Author

Ty Wiggins is a leadership expert who is committed to ensuring new CEOs are set up for success. As the global lead of Russell Reynolds Associates' CEO & Executive Transition Practice, he is a trusted advisor to world-leading CEOs, helping them to successfully transition into their roles to unlock business and personal success faster. Ty is one of only a handful of people globally with a Ph.D. in senior leadership transitions. He harnesses his deep academic, consulting, and coaching background to provide CEOs, boards, and senior leaders across industries with the advice, support, challenge, and insight needed to start well and perform quickly.

Index